Daniel

GOD'S PATTERN
FOR THE FUTURE

BIBLE STUDY GUIDE

From the Bible-teaching ministry of

Charles R. Swindoll

INSIGHT FOR LIVING

Chuck graduated in 1963 from Dallas Theological Seminary, where he now serves as the school's fourth president, helping to prepare a new generation of men and women for the ministry. Chuck has served in pastorates in three states: Massachusetts, Texas, and California, including almost twenty-three years at the First Evangelical Free Church in Fullerton, California. His sermon messages have been aired over radio since 1979 as the *Insight for Living* broadcast. A best-selling author, Chuck has written numerous books and booklets on many subjects.

Based on the outlines and transcripts of Chuck's sermons, the study guide text is co-authored by Bryce Klabunde, a graduate of Biola University and Dallas Theological Seminary. He also wrote the Living Insights sections.

Editor in Chief:
Cynthia Swindoll

Coauthor of Text:
Bryce Klabunde

Assistant Editor:
Wendy Peterson

Copy Editor:
Deborah Gibbs

Text Designer:
Gary Lett

Graphic System Administrator:
Bob Haskins

Director, Communications Division:
Deedee Snyder

Creative Services Manager:
John Norton

Project Coordinator:
Colette Muse

Printer:
Sinclair Printing Company

Unless otherwise identified, all Scripture references are from the New American Standard Bible, © The Lockman Foundation 1960, 1962, 1963, 1968, 1971, 1972, 1973, 1975, 1977. Used by permission. The other translation cited is the *Amplified Bible* [AMPLIFIED].

ISBN 0-8499-8734-2
COVER DESIGN: Gary Lett
COVER ILLUSTRATION: *Daniel's Answer to the King* by Briton Riviere.
Printed in the United States of America

CONTENTS

INTRODUCTION

Daniel, the prophet, could be called a man for all seasons. He "stood in the gap" through one pagan ruler after another, never once compromising his convictions. As one in great authority, Daniel certainly had opportunities to fudge morally, spiritually, and ethically . . . but that peerless model of integrity never did.

These studies, however, are about more than the man himself. They also deal with some of the most colorful and significant prophetic themes found in Scripture. What the book of Revelation is to the New Testament, Daniel is to the Old. With sweeping, broad brush strokes of his pen, Daniel covers the major areas of prophecy.

As you read each lesson in this study guide, with your Bible open to this great book, may God stimulate and strengthen you. My hope is that you will do more than just learn about a few interesting events regarding the future, important though they may be . . . but that Daniel's example of integrity will mark your life in a permanent manner.

Chuck Swindoll

Chuck Swindoll

PUTTING TRUTH
INTO ACTION

Knowledge apart from application falls short of God's desire for His children. He wants us to apply what we learn so that we will change and grow. This study guide was prepared with these goals in mind. As you go through the following pages, we hope your desire to discover biblical truth will grow as your understanding of God's Word increases and that you will be encouraged to apply what you've learned.

To assist you in your study, we've included a section called **Living Insights** at the end of each lesson. These exercises will challenge you to study further and to think of specific ways to put your discoveries into action.

On occasion a lesson is followed by a **Digging Deeper** section, which gives you additional information and resources to probe further into some issues raised in that lesson.

There are many ways to use this guide—in personal devotions, group studies, discussions with friends and family, and Sunday school classes. And, of course, it's an ideal study aid when you're listening to its corresponding *Insight for Living* radio series.

To benefit most from this study guide, we would encourage you to consider it a spiritual journal. That's why we've included space in the **Living Insights** for recording your thoughts and discoveries. We hope you'll return to those sections often for review and encouragement as you continue to grow in your walk with Christ.

Bryce Klabunde
Coauthor of Text
Author of Living Insights

Daniel

GOD'S PATTERN
FOR THE FUTURE

SURVEY OF DANIEL

BIOGRAPHICAL SECTION

Daniel Interprets the King's Dreams
Main Emphasis: Daniel the Prophet

Outline

Chapter 1: Introduction and Setting

Chapter 2: Nebuchadnezzar's Major Dream

Chapters 3–6: Historical Narratives
(political and personal)

Chapters 1 through 6

PROPHETIC SECTION

Angel Interprets Daniel's Dreams
Main Emphasis: The Prophecies of Daniel

Outline

Chapter 7: Daniel's Major Vision

Chapter 8–12: Prophetic Visions
(near and far)

Chapters 7 through 12

Political Powers in Daniel's Day . . . . and Afterward . . . .

<u>Babylonian Rule</u>
Nebuchadnezzar
Belshazzar

<u>Medo-Persian Rule</u>
Darius the Mede
Cyrus, King of Persia

<u>Grecian Rule</u>
Alexander the Great
Four Generals

<u>Roman Rule</u>
Last of the
Gentile Powers

Chapter 1

PROPHECY IN PANORAMA

Selected Scriptures

What is happening to our world? As we watch the news, we see that another earthquake has turned a metropolis into rubble. The latest hurricane has ripped through a coastal town. Another wildfire has charred acres of forestland. Record-breaking rains flood one region while crop-withering drought bakes another. The fabric of nature seems to be tearing apart at the seams . . . and with it, the fabric of society.

> The population is exploding.
> Economies are collapsing.
> Ethnic groups are battling.

In these tumultuous times, Christ's prophetic words ring with particular relevance:

> "You will be hearing of wars and rumors of wars; see that you are not frightened, for those things must take place, but that is not yet the end. For nation will rise against nation, and kingdom against kingdom, and in various places there will be famines and earthquakes. But all these things are merely the beginning of birth pangs." (Matt. 24:6–8)

Merely the beginning. As the end approaches, wars will escalate and disasters will strike harder and faster. Even so, Jesus encourages us not to be afraid. How can He say that? Because He understands the whole scope of God's redemptive plan. He sees the sunlight beyond the storm, and He is confident that the ship carrying God's people will make it through.

How confident are you about the future? Does the chaos of our

1

times have you biting your nails? To calm our worries about the future is one reason God gave us Daniel. This prophetic book teaches us that God is in control of human affairs, no matter what disasters may rock our world.

Introductory Matters

As we begin our study of Daniel and his prophecies, we need to acknowledge several realities about the subject of prophecy in general.

First, *people are hungry for prophetic information.* Have you noticed the rising popularity of mediums and clairvoyants? Movies and TV shows regularly make heroes out of psychics who are "in tune" with the spirit world. And even in these scientific times, many people still map out their lives with a horoscope in hand. People are hungry for spiritual guidance; unfortunately, they are feeding themselves poison. We need to return to the true source of information about the future, the Bible.

Second, *there is a great imbalance among prophecy students.* Some prophecy students neglect the rest of God's Word and study nothing but prophecy. Their imbalance reveals itself as they set dates for Christ's coming and maintain a smug, know-it-all attitude. However, God gave us prophecy not to tickle our curiosity about tomorrow, but to motivate us to live for Him today, to keep us pure and energize our faith. We need a fresh approach to prophecy, one that remains balanced.

Third, *prophecy is a frequent theme in the Bible.* It is a solid stone in the foundation of our faith. The New Testament alone refers to Christ's return about 318 times in 260 chapters.[1]

On the whole, the two great books that contain specific end-times prophecy are Daniel, which emphasizes the Gentiles, and Revelation, which emphasizes the Jews. What Revelation is to the New Testament, Daniel is to the Old. Jesus Himself referred to Daniel's prophecy in Matthew 24:15, and the gospel writer underscored its significance by adding: "let the reader take notice *and* ponder *and* consider *and* heed [this]" (AMPLIFIED).

To better understand Daniel's message, we must first see how his visions fit into the overall scheme of prophecy. The chart on the following page will be our guide as we walk through the major eras and events of prophetic history.

---

1. Robert D. Foster, *The Challenge* newsletter, November 15, 1975.

PROPHECY IN PANORAMA

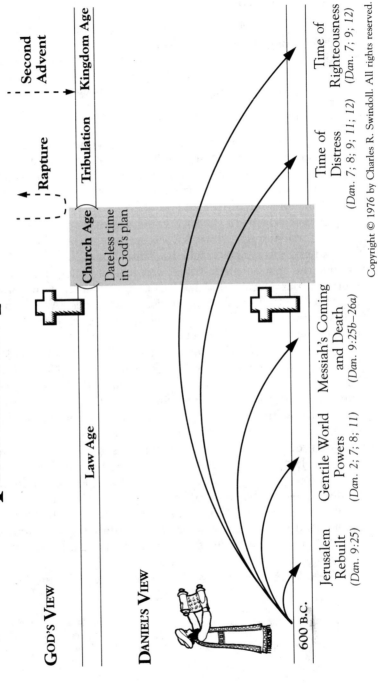

GOD'S VIEW

Law Age | (Church Age) Dateless time in God's plan | Rapture | Tribulation | Second Advent | Kingdom Age

DANIEL'S VIEW

600 B.C.

Jerusalem Rebuilt (*Dan. 9:25*) | Gentile World Powers (*Dan. 2; 7; 8; 11*) | Messiah's Coming and Death (*Dan. 9:25b–26a*) | Time of Distress (*Dan. 7; 8; 9; 11; 12*) | Time of Righteousness (*Dan. 7; 9; 12*)

God's Overall Scheme

The top half of the chart represents God's strategy for the world, conceived long before He molded creation's first clay. Through centuries of progressive revelation, God has unveiled His marvelous plan to the authors of Scripture. Let's look at several of the key stages that will help us see where we've been and where we're headed.

The Law

The first era on the chart, the Law, began on forbidding Mount Sinai. There God gave Moses the Ten Commandments and a long list of instructions for holy living. From the days of Adam and Eve, God had spoken to individuals directly, but now His Word was etched in stone for all to read and obey.

Under God's hand, Israel became a great nation and gained international respect. However, except for a few golden eras of faithfulness, the people rebelled against God. Civil war split the nation; the ten northern tribes were called Israel, and the two southern tribes became Judah. Both nations murdered His messengers, broke His Law, and worshiped pagan gods. After years of patient restraint, God finally handed them over to foreign powers to reap the harvest of destruction they had sown.

In 722 B.C., Assyria defeated Israel; and in 586 B.C. the Babylonians finished off Judah, razing Solomon's splendid temple and hauling the people away in chains to Babylon. Among the first exiles to be deported was promising young Daniel. He became a model of how the Jews should live in captivity, serving the Babylonian kings with integrity while remaining devoted to God.

After seventy years of captivity, caravans of Jews were allowed to return to Jerusalem and start rebuilding the temple, fulfilling Jeremiah's prophecy (see Jer. 25:11–12; 29:10; see also Isa. 44:26, 28).[2] Under the leadership of Ezra and Nehemiah, the city walls were mended in 445 B.C. With temple worship reestablished, the city rebuilt, and a government in operation, Israel was a nation once more, though often under the dominion of Gentile powers. But God's people never worshiped idols again.

The Old Testament closes with Malachi warning the Jews not

---

2. The seventy years in Jeremiah's prophecy can be calculated either from the date the first exiles left in 605 B.C. to the start of the temple rebuilding project in 536 B.C., or from the destruction of Jerusalem in 586 B.C. to the completion of the temple in 516 B.C.

to repeat the mistakes that led to their destruction. Four hundred years passed with no fresh word from the Lord. Then, suddenly, the silence was shattered by "the voice of one crying in the wilderness": John the Baptist was announcing the coming of Jesus the Messiah (Matt. 3:3).

Living and ministering in the Law era, Jesus did what no one else could do: He perfectly fulfilled God's righteous demands. And through His death and resurrection, Christ atoned for the sins of all Law-breakers, ushering in an age of grace.

The Church

The Church Age was hidden behind a curtain of mystery to the Old Testament prophets, including Daniel. Jesus pulled back the veil when He announced He would build His church, and even "the gates of Hades shall not overpower it" (Matt. 16:18). Christ's church-building project began at Pentecost, when the Holy Spirit descended on the believers in Jerusalem (Acts 2).

This new program is completely different in lifestyle and philosophy than the age of the Law. No longer are the Jews the only recipients of God's Word. No longer is the temple the only place to receive divine mercy. No longer are people shackled to the rigid requirements of the Law. Christ has set believers free and empowered them with the Holy Spirit. He has unlocked the promises of God, swinging open the door of salvation to all people.

> There is neither Jew nor Greek, there is neither slave nor free man, there is neither male nor female; for you are all one in Christ Jesus. (Gal. 3:28; see also Eph. 1–3)

We don't know how long the Church Age will last, but we do know that it will end at the Rapture, when Christ returns to gather up His followers in the clouds.

The Rapture

Christ has pledged that He would come again some day (John 14:1–3). Paul describes that glorious day:

> For the Lord Himself will descend from heaven with a shout, with the voice of the archangel, and with the trumpet of God; and the dead in Christ shall rise first. Then we who are alive and remain shall

be caught up together with them in the clouds to meet the Lord in the air, and thus we shall always be with the Lord. Therefore comfort one another with these words. (1 Thess. 4:16–18)

"In the twinkling of an eye," all who have trusted Christ for their salvation—both living and dead—will exchange their old, earthly bodies for new, heavenly ones (1 Cor. 15:51–54). As a result, we will escape the "hour of testing" that God has planned for the world (see Rev. 3:10). What hope!

The Tribulation

Unbelievers left behind at the Rapture will enter a period Daniel calls "a time of distress" (Dan. 12:1).[3] The Scriptures paint a horrifying picture of this seven-year span (see Matt. 24:21–24; Rev. 13–19). It begins with a world leader (the Beast) and his right-hand man (the False Prophet) using satanic power to deceive and control the nations (see Rev. 13:1–2). Together, the two will rule the world politically, economically, and religiously.

According to Daniel 9:27, the evil dictator "will make a firm covenant" with the Jews in Israel, agreeing to let them alone. Peace will settle on the earth for a while, but the dictator will break his agreement in the middle of the Tribulation period and crush anyone who opposes his supreme authority. In Revelation, we are even told that he will only allow those with the mark of the Beast to have any economic freedom (13:17). Those who have become Christians during this time will be cruelly persecuted, and many will die.

However, the Lord will allow evil to reign for only so long. He will pour out the boiling cauldron of His wrath, searing the earth with a series of judgments that will culminate in the Battle of Armageddon (Rev. 6–18).

The Second Advent

When all the armies of the world have assembled at the plain of Armageddon, Christ will return to earth, this time not as a tiny baby but as a mighty warrior (Rev. 19:11–21; see also Matt. 24:29–31). His armies will include all the raptured saints. With swift retribution, He will conquer His foes and throw the Beast and the False

---

3. Additional Scriptures relating to the "time of distress" are Daniel 2:35, 44; 7:7–12, 19–25; 8:9–12, 23–25; 9:27; 11:36–12:1a; 12:6–7, 11–12.

Prophet "alive into the lake of fire which burns with brimstone" (Rev. 19:20). Judgment of the world will follow, as He separates the "sheep" from the "goats," believers from unbelievers (Matt. 25:31–46). Then He will bind Satan for a thousand years (Rev. 20:1–3) and commence a magnificent, heaven-on-earth age called the millennial kingdom—an age humankind has dreamed about since the Garden of Eden.

The Millennial Kingdom

During this thousand-year period, God will honor the promises that He made to David and his descendants (see 2 Sam. 7:8–17). The Son of David, Jesus Himself, will rule the earth in true righteousness and peace (see Isa. 11:1–9). The surviving Tribulation saints, including a large remnant of Jews, will enter the kingdom and enjoy long and happy lives, living in a perfect world (Rev. 20:1–6).

However, life in paradise doesn't guarantee sinless character. Not all who are born during this time will trust Christ. At the end of the thousand years, God will release Satan, and he will deceive many people. The ultimate battle between good and evil will occur, pitting the forces of Satan against the people of God (Rev. 20:7–9). Fire from heaven will devour the wicked once and for all, and the Devil will be thrown into the lake of fire to "be tormented day and night forever and ever" (v. 10).[4]

A New Heaven and a New Earth

With evil vanquished, God will resurrect the dead and usher them before His Great White Throne for one final judgment (see vv. 11–15). He will destroy the old heaven and earth in a fiery cataclysm and create "a new heaven and a new earth" (21:1), in which His redeemed people will dwell with Him forever. In this pristine new world, free from sin's curse, the Lord will

> "wipe away every tear from their eyes; and there
> shall no longer be any death; there shall no longer
> be any mourning, or crying, or pain; the first things
> have passed away." (21:4)

Daniel's Specific Scope

From his limited vantage point, Daniel didn't foresee all of the

---

4. Other Scriptures foretelling the millennial kingdom are Daniel 12 and Isaiah 40–66.

plains and valleys of God's plan, but he did observe five mountain peaks: (1) the rebuilding of Jerusalem, (2) the rise and fall of several Gentile nations, (3) the coming and death of the Messiah, (4) the time of trouble, and (5) the time of righteousness. Most of Daniel's prophetic dreams have already been fulfilled in history. Only the last two events rise before us now.

Our Basic Response

We are living in a unique point on God's timeline. Unlike the days of Daniel, nothing remains to be fulfilled before God sets in motion the end times events. That fact should start our thoughts spinning: *What if Christ returns today? Am I ready? Am I sure that I would escape God's wrath?* Now is the moment to make sure. Place your faith in Jesus Christ, who died on the cross to make atonement for your sins and who rose again to guarantee your own future resurrection to glory.

The apostle Paul penned God's promise to those who believe:

> There is therefore now no condemnation for
> those who are in Christ Jesus. (Rom. 8:1)

Clinging to that promise, our fear of facing God melts into anticipation. What joy it will be to feel the eternal embrace of our Savior. Come, Lord Jesus. Come!

 Living Insights

One of the purposes of prophecy is to give us hope. In his book *The End: What Jesus Really Said about the Last Things*, A. J. Conyers defines the virtue of hope as "a willing, trusting anticipation of what God will do."[5]

What will God do when He bursts through earth's front door? For starters, He'll restore justice—no more criminals getting off the hook. He'll put an end to evil and suffering. He'll create the perfect world we've been dreaming about. Best of all, He'll give us His presence. After such a long wait, His children will finally get to see their Father.

---

5. A. J. Conyers, *The End: What Jesus Really Said about the Last Things* (Downers Grove, Ill.: InterVarsity Press, 1995), pp. 50–51.

Does the thought of His coming fill you with anticipation? What do you long for the most?

_____

_____

_____

According to 1 John 3:1–2, what was John anticipating about the Lord's return?

_____

_____

Anticipation energizes us. For example, have you ever put off cleaning your house . . . and put it off . . . and put if off . . . until you find out a favorite relative is coming? Suddenly, you become a whirling, cleansing machine. _Vrooom_ goes the vacuum; _plop_ goes the mop; _fluster_ goes the feather duster. The house is cleaned in record time.

What self-cleansing effect does the anticipation of Christ's coming produce in us (see v. 3)?

_____

_____

Anticipation is like a mountain spring bubbling inside us. According to the following verses, what other effects flow out of it?

Isaiah 40:31 _____

Romans 15:13 _____

2 Peter 3:11–14_____

Prophecy gives us hope; hope fills us with anticipation; anticipation energizes us to live for the Lord today.

Keep that goal in mind as you study the prophecies in Daniel. God doesn't give us knowledge about the future so we can stand around speculating on the time of His arrival. He gives us prophecy to motivate us. To encourage us. To change us.

Are you ready for change?

Chapter 2

How to Pass a Test Without Cheating
Daniel 1

Tests of character are the toughest tests to pass. Tougher than state bar exams, medical boards, and orals for a Ph.D. all rolled into one.

Why? Because when our integrity is on the line, we must go beyond mere knowledge and dig deep to the very bedrock of who we are. Character tests expose our hidden flaws; but they also reveal our strengths—our determination to love, our commitment to honesty, our faith in God.

In the first chapter of Daniel, we'll see a young man stripped of every external support of his faith and identity in God. Few of us have ever or will ever face such a test. Daniel, though, emerges not only with his beliefs intact but with a character that will shine God's light throughout his life. Let's see how he did it.

Historical Setting

Daniel himself relates the historical backdrop to his story.

> In the third year of the reign of Jehoiakim king of Judah, Nebuchadnezzar king of Babylon came to Jerusalem and besieged it. And the Lord gave Jehoiakim king of Judah into his hand, along with some of the vessels of the house of God; and he brought them to the land of Shinar, to the house of his god, and he brought the vessels into the treasury of his god. (Dan. 1:1–2)

Having soundly defeated the Egyptians at Carchemish in 605 B.C., Nebuchadnezzar rode the wave of victory southward through Syria and Palestine, swallowing up smaller nations like Judah. The assault on Jerusalem resulted in Jehoiakim's quick surrender and an agreement that Judah would be a vassal state.[1]

---

1. Nebuchadnezzar would strike Jerusalem twice more. In 597 B.C., he would stamp out a rebellion, plunder treasure, and deport Jehoiachin (Jehoiakim's son and successor), along with thousands of other Jews. In 586 B.C., he would brutalize Jehoiachin's successor, Zedekiah, and decimate Jerusalem, wiping out Judah as a nation (see 2 Kings 24:8–25:21; Lam. 4).

This was a major turning point in Hebrew history, for it marked the beginning of "the times of the Gentiles"—a period in which Gentile nations would dominate the land (see Luke 21:24) and no king from David's line would sit on Israel's throne.[2]

At the Second Advent, however, Christ will restore Israel as a glorious nation as He ushers in the millennial kingdom. The following chart illustrates this overall historical scheme.

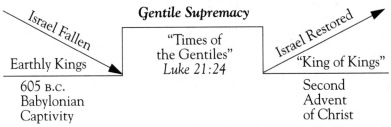

The first Gentile king to trample Jerusalem underfoot was Nebuchadnezzar, who helped himself to some of the temple treasures and selected a group of Judah's finest young men to be taken to Babylon as his private servants.

This is where Daniel enters the scene.

Facing the Test

Chosen for deportation, Daniel describes the selection process and what happened when he arrived at his new home in distant Babylon.

The Choice

> Then the king ordered Ashpenaz, the chief of his officials, to bring in some of the sons of Israel, including some of the royal family and of the nobles, youths in whom was no defect, who were good-looking, showing intelligence in every branch of wisdom, endowed with understanding, and discerning knowledge, and who had ability for serving in the king's court. (Dan. 1:3–4a)

---

2. See J. Dwight Pentecost, "Daniel," *The Bible Knowledge Commentary*, Old Testament edition, ed. John F. Walvoord and Roy B. Zuck (Wheaton, Ill.: Scripture Press, Victor Books, 1985), p. 1329.

"Skim off the cream" was the command to Ashpenaz. Nebuchadnezzar wanted the best that Judah had to offer as examples of his conquering power. They were to be youths (teenagers), physically fit, handsome, and sharp-minded. Young Daniel qualified, and so did Hananiah, Mishael, and Azariah (v. 6).

The Course

The king ordered Ashpenaz to

> teach them the literature and language of the Chaldeans. And the king appointed for them a daily ration from the king's choice food and from the wine which he drank, and appointed that they should be educated three years, at the end of which they were to enter the king's personal service. (vv. 4b–5)

Total indoctrination was the objective. Nebuchadnezzar wanted these boys to walk, talk, and think Babylonian-style. So right away they were enrolled in a three-year liberal arts program that "probably included a study of agriculture, architecture, astrology, astronomy, law, mathematics, and the difficult Akkadian language."[3] The royal diet would strengthen their bodies for this task. However, as commentator H. C. Leupold points out, there was more to the meals than nourishment.

> All meals served at the king's table were feasts, and among the heathen feasts were feasts in honor of the gods. . . . To share in such a feast was the equivalent of honoring such an idol, admitting his claims and existence, and so practically denying the one true God.[4]

Even the food and drink were meant to compromise their convictions.

The king, you see, was determined to replace the boys' Jewish values with Babylonian values. Everything familiar had been taken away—their families, their homes, their religion. According to the Jewish historian Josephus, the Babylonians even made them eunuchs,

---

3. Pentecost, "Daniel," p. 1330.

4. H. C. Leupold, *Exposition of Daniel* (1949; reprint, Grand Rapids, Mich.: Baker Book House, 1969), p. 66.

which, if true, explains why Daniel never married.[5]

The final blow came when they took away their identities. Their God-honoring Hebrew names were replaced with pagan names that honored the Babylonian gods.

> Then the commander of the officials assigned new names to them; and to Daniel he assigned the name Belteshazzar, to Hananiah Shadrach, to Mishael Meshach, and to Azariah Abed-nego. (v. 7)

Imagine a fourteen- or fifteen-year-old boy living hundreds of miles from his family, forced to take college-level courses in a foreign language, constantly barraged by pagan philosophy, and surrounded by the intimidating sights and sounds of a big city. There's no going home. No summer vacation. Only day in, day out brainwashing in the ways of the world. It would be quite a test of his beliefs, wouldn't it? Daniel not only handled the test but passed it with flying colors.

Passing the Test

Four factors contributed to Daniel's ability to stand firm: (1) his inner convictions, (2) a wise approach, (3) divine assistance, and (4) some unique distinctions.

Inner Convictions

For the first factor, we must look deep into Daniel's thoughts and spirit, where the bricks of strong character are formed.

> But Daniel made up his mind that he would not defile himself with the king's choice food or with the wine which he drank. (v. 8a)

Literally, Daniel "set upon his heart" that he would not defile himself by eating the unclean food. He didn't wait until the banquet was spread before him to decide. He made up his mind *before* the delicious smells tantalized his teenage appetite.

In the private chamber of his heart, he set up a wall-like resolve that he would not compromise. What did he use as foundation material? The scriptural lessons he had learned at home and that

---

5. Josephus, *The Antiquities of the Jews*, in *Josephus: Complete Works*, trans. William Whiston (Grand Rapids, Mich.: Kregel Publications, 1978), book X, p. 222. See also Isaiah 39:7, where the word translated *officials* in the NASB is rendered *eunuchs* in the NIV.

had been handed down from the reformations of King Josiah and the teachings of the great prophets Jeremiah, Habakkuk, and Zephaniah.

The word of the Lord was unmistakable: "I am the Lord your God. Consecrate yourselves therefore, and be holy; for I am holy" (Lev. 11:44). Daniel may have been living in an unclean world, but he was determined to remain clean.

Wise Approach

Having made his resolution, Daniel "sought permission from the commander of the officials that he might not defile himself" (Dan. 1:8b). His approach showed great wisdom. He could have defied the commander's orders and refused to eat. Instead, he built a bridge of understanding between himself and his superior. He pleaded passionately to not defile himself; then he listened to the commander's point of view:

> "I am afraid of my lord the king, who has appointed your food and your drink; for why should he see your faces looking more haggard than the youths who are your own age? Then you would make me forfeit my head to the king." (v. 10)

Sensitive to his supervisor's dilemma, Daniel proposed a ten-day trial:

> "Please test your servants for ten days, and let us be given some vegetables to eat and water to drink. Then let our appearance be observed in your presence, and the appearance of the youths who are eating the king's choice food; and deal with your servants according to what you see." (vv. 12–13)

Daniel didn't let his convictions put the commander on the spot. Rather, he respected the commander and his situation by leaving him with the final say. How could Daniel take this risk? Because of his faith in the God who honors those who honor Him. Daniel's wisdom was based on the fact that God is in control.

Divine Assistance

From the opening curtain of this drama, God has been the unseen director, setting the scenes and guiding the players through their parts. According to verse 2, King Nebuchadnezzar didn't conquer

Jerusalem—"The *Lord* gave Jehoiakim king of Judah into his hand" (emphasis added). And according to verse 9, it was God inside the commander's heart who was softening him toward Daniel:

> Now God granted Daniel favor and compassion in the sight of the commander of the officials. (v. 9)

Later in the story, the Lord became like a private tutor for the Hebrew youths:

> God gave them knowledge and intelligence in every branch of literature and wisdom; Daniel even understood all kinds of visions and dreams. (v. 17)

Although the Jewish captives were living under the shadow of divine discipline, separated from the land of promise and the temple, God had not abandoned them. His hand was moving silently in the thoughts and feelings of Jews and non-Jews alike, changing attitudes, affecting decisions, and, as a result, altering history.

In Daniel and his friends' case, God made "even [their] enemies to be at peace with [them]" (Prov. 16:7).

> And at the end of ten days their appearance seemed better and they were fatter than all the youths who had been eating the king's choice food. So the overseer continued to withhold their choice food and the wine they were to drink, and kept giving them vegetables. (Dan. 1:15–16)

Unique Distinctions

Because Daniel stood by his principles and trusted God for the results, God honored him with some special talents and distinctions that would sustain him for the rest of his life.

> Then at the end of the days which the king had specified for presenting them, the commander of the officials presented them before Nebuchadnezzar. And the king talked with them, and out of them all not one was found like Daniel, Hananiah, Mishael and Azariah; so they entered the king's personal service. And as for every matter of wisdom and understanding about which the king consulted them, he found them ten times better than all the magicians and conjurers who were in all his realm. And

15

Daniel continued until the first year of Cyrus the king. (vv. 18–21)

Nebuchadnezzar had chosen young Daniel to demonstrate Babylonian power and supremacy. Ironically, though, Daniel outlived Nebuchadnezzar, his successors, and even the empire. He lived until the days of Cyrus, ruler of the Medes and Persians. And he lives on today, as a reminder that God's realm is higher and more supreme than that of any king.

Abiding Principles

As we review Daniel's story, two principles stand out. First, *inner conviction can overcome any outer pressure*. Why? Because the power of God is on our side. The key to tapping into that power is making up our minds like Daniel did, *before* the luscious aroma of the temptation swirls in front of us.

Second, *God-honoring convictions yield God-given rewards*. Daniel had no power over his circumstances or the people around him, but there was one thing he did have power over—his reaction to these influences. Within that small circle of control, he chose to be a man of integrity and conviction, to honor God with his mind and body. And he let the Lord take care of the things in the larger circle— his superior, his education, his health, and his rewards in life.

May we be as wise as Daniel . . . and live as faithfully.

 Living Insights

We all know what it's like to live in Babylon. Nearly every day we are confronted with the idols of money, youth, sex, power, fame, and political correctness. So how can we live *in* Babylon without becoming a part *of* Babylon? Just as Daniel did, by following inner convictions we've set our hearts upon.

How strong are your convictions? Can you rely on them to hold up under pressure?

_____

_____

_____

What areas of your life might be straining under Babylon's pressure and need to be reinforced?

_____

_____

_____

What decision(s) do you need to make before you get into a compromising situation?

_____

_____

_____

Does this decision involve someone else, as Daniel's did the commander? Your boss, a friend, a family member?

_____

What wise approach can you use to explain your convictions to this person? When would be a good time?

_____

_____

_____

It probably wasn't easy for Daniel and his companions to turn down the king's choice food. And it's not going to be easy for you to stick to your convictions either. So express to the Lord your need for His divine assistance and pray for Him to work in the hearts of those involved.

_____

_____

_____

_____

Chapter 3

A KING ON THE COUCH

Daniel 2:1–30

C ould you use some encouragement that God is still in control
of world events, including every aspect of your personal life?
That His Word is as reliable as ever? That He is still faithful to His
people? That He hears your prayers? That He can still be trusted
with your life—even during the darkest of times?

"That's a dream," you might say, especially if you're struggling
spiritually right now. And you would be partially right. For we can
learn all these great truths from chapter 2 of Daniel, where God
invades the dreams of King Nebuchadnezzar to reveal Himself and
His plan for the ages. So read on. One man's insomnia is another
man's instruction.

Historical Backdrop

To better appreciate God's interruption of Nebuchadnezzar's
slumber, let's get some historical background.

A Resplendent City

Nebuchadnezzar, remember, is king of Babylon, the dominant
world power of its day and captor of the Jews. Writing about this ancient
city and its king, Merrill F. Unger helps us picture the grandeur:

> Nebuchadnezzar's brilliant city included vast fortifi-
> cations, famous streets like the Processional, canals,
> temples and palaces. The Ishtar Gate led through
> the double wall of fortifications and was adorned
> with rows of bulls and dragons in colored enameled
> brick. Nebuchadnezzar's throne room was likewise
> adorned with enameled bricks. . . . Not far distant
> were the hanging gardens, which to the Greeks were
> one of the seven wonders of the world. How well
> the words of Dan. 4:30 fit this ambitious builder: "Is
> not this great Babylon, which I have built for the
> royal dwelling place by the might of my power and
> to the glory of my majesty?"[1]

1. Merrill F. Unger, *Unger's Bible Dictionary*, 3d ed. (Chicago, Ill.: Moody Press, 1966), p. 115.

Into this world of pomp, protection, and pride comes a message from the Lord of Hosts. But He doesn't deliver it with an army of angels or fire from heaven. He drops it into a dream. And a sleeping king meets the King who never sleeps.

A Recurring Dream

> Now in the second year of the reign of Nebuchadnezzar, Nebuchadnezzar had dreams; and his spirit was troubled and his sleep left him. (2:1)

Compare the plural *dreams* in verse 1 with the singular *dream* in verse 3. Apparently, the king has been dreaming the same dream over and over again, which plagues him with worry and insomnia. Disturbed, he seeks an interpretation from his advisors.

> Then the king gave orders to call in the magicians, the conjurers, the sorcerers and the Chaldeans, to tell the king his dreams. So they came in and stood before the king. And the king said to them, "I had a dream, and my spirit is anxious to understand the dream." (vv. 2–3)

What a collection of mystics! Shirley MacLaine, eat your heart out. If anyone can harvest the political or spiritual meaning from a field of dreams, certainly this group can. Or can they?

The Search for an Interpretation

A desperate search for the dream's meaning begins with this august assembly of soothsayers. You can almost see them falling all over each other like a pack of puppies eager for their master's praise. This is a golden opportunity to get in good with the king.

The Confident Counselors

The counselors appear neither surprised nor bewildered by Nebuchadnezzar's request. Rather, they are confident that, with their collective wisdom, they can discern the dream's meaning.

> Then the Chaldeans spoke to the king in Aramaic:[2] "O king, live forever! Tell the dream to your

---

2. Although Akkadian was most likely the language of the intellectual elite, Aramaic was the common language of the Gentile world. See *The Eerdmans Bible Dictionary*, ed. Allen C. Myers (Grand Rapids, Mich.: William B. Eerdmans Publishing Co., 1987), p. 71.

servants, and we will declare the interpretation." (v. 4)

Knowing that anyone can fabricate an interpretation once the dream is disclosed, the king isn't satisfied with their response. So he decides to put them to the test.

> The king answered and said to the Chaldeans, "The command from me is firm: if you do not make known to me the dream and its interpretation, you will be torn limb from limb, and your houses will be made a rubbish heap. But if you declare the dream and its interpretation, you will receive from me gifts and a reward and great honor; therefore declare to me the dream and its interpretation." (vv. 5–6)

"If you're worth your salt, you'll not only interpret the dream, you'll tell me *what* I dreamed. Or else." Since they don't have the answer, these "wise men" do the wisest thing they can under the circumstances—stall (v. 7).

But Nebuchadnezzar isn't fooled.

> The king answered and said, "I know for certain that you are bargaining for time, inasmuch as you have seen that the command from me is firm, that if you do not make the dream known to me, there is only one decree for you. For you have agreed together to speak lying and corrupt words before me until the situation is changed; therefore tell me the dream, that I may know that you can declare to me its interpretation." (vv. 8–9)

Cornered by the king, they can do nothing but admit their inadequacy.

> The Chaldeans answered the king and said, "There is not a man on earth who could declare the matter for the king, inasmuch as no great king or ruler has ever asked anything like this of any magician, conjurer or Chaldean. Moreover, the thing which the king demands is difficult, and there is no one else who could declare it to the king except gods, whose dwelling place is not with mortal flesh." (vv. 10–11)

For those who might have some interest in the occult, take

note. Fortune tellers, mediums, astrologers, and psychics may stir up a lot of fear and curiosity. They may try to supplant God and distort His Word. They may even, like the court magicians in Moses' day, appear to possess the power of God. But they cannot do what only God can do. They cannot discern the depths of His counsel, communicate His heart, or reveal His program.

Sovereignty and sorcery are as far apart as heaven and hell.

The King's Deadly Decree

Angered by the ignorance of his advisors, Nebuchadnezzar pronounces a death sentence on all the "wise men" of Babylon. Included in that group are Daniel and his friends (vv. 12–13; see also 1:20; 5:11–12).

Daniel the Interpreter

With Daniel's entrance, our story takes a courageous turn.

A Question for the Captain

The king's captain, Arioch, arrives to execute Daniel. What would you do at this point? Panic? Run? Shift the attention to your friends? Look at Daniel's response.

> Then Daniel replied with discretion and discernment to Arioch, the captain of the king's bodyguard, who had gone forth to slay the wise men of Babylon; he answered and said to Arioch, the king's commander, "For what reason is the decree from the king so urgent?" Then Arioch informed Daniel about the matter. (vv. 14–15)

Beautiful. Some Christians think the only sensible response to unjust secular authority is brash rebellion. Not Daniel. He has the courage to probe and the confidence in God to offer an alternative. Yet he expresses these with self-control and wisdom.

The result? Not only does Arioch refrain from executing Daniel, he explains the king's dilemma and then apparently takes Daniel before the king. Catch it now—Nebuchadnezzar's head henchman appears before the king with the man he should have killed. More amazingly, Nebuchadnezzar listens to Daniel and gives him time to discover the interpretation (v. 16). Is God in control here, or what?

Waiting in Prayer

Why did Daniel want more time? To seek God in prayer.

> Then Daniel went to his house and informed his friends, Hananiah, Mishael and Azariah, about the matter, in order that they might request compassion from the God of heaven concerning this mystery, so that Daniel and his friends might not be destroyed with the rest of the wise men of Babylon. (vv. 17–18)

What a predicament. No one can interpret the dream, not even Daniel. Apparently, some wise men of Babylon have already lost their lives. And Daniel and his friends could be the next to die. Hopeless? No. It's the perfect opportunity for God to work on behalf of those who trust in Him.

When you get to the end of your own ability, when you don't know the answer and the clock is ticking, it doesn't mean that God is idle. Rather, He often puts us in situations in which only He is sufficient. Daniel knew that. So he prayed with his friends . . . and waited on the Lord (see also Ps. 27:14; Isa. 30:18; 40:31; Rom. 8:25).

Pausing for Praise

At His appointed time, God graciously reveals Nebuchadnezzar's dream and its interpretation to Daniel in a vision (Dan. 2:19). At this point, most of us would probably leap out of bed, dive into a robe, and bolt for the king's palace. "I've got it, I've got it," we would shout, banging on the king's door. But Daniel pauses to acknowledge the Giver of the interpretation.

> Daniel answered and said,
> "Let the name of God be blessed forever and ever,
> For wisdom and power belong to Him.
> And it is He who changes the times and the epochs;
> He removes kings and establishes kings;
> He gives wisdom to wise men,
> And knowledge to men of understanding.
> It is He who reveals the profound and hidden things;
> He knows what is in the darkness,
> And the light dwells with Him.

To Thee, O God of my fathers, I give thanks
and praise,
For Thou hast given me wisdom and power;
Even now Thou hast made known to me what
we requested of Thee,
For Thou hast made known to us the king's
matter." (vv. 20–23)

Four verses of solid, specific praise! How often do we respond
to God's blessings that way? When God intervenes in our lives,
we're sometimes tempted to grab a little glory for ourselves, take
credit for the outcome. Or we may simply take God for granted
and forget to thank Him. Not Daniel. He knows that without God
there would be no interpretation, no wisdom, no audience with the
king. In fact, there would be no kings and countries at all if God
did not will it. Praise reminds us how capable and gracious our God
is. It reminds us that, without Him, we can do nothing (see also
Heb. 13:15).

Standing before the King

Prayer. Revelation. Praise. Now it's time to see the king (Dan.
2:24). Arioch takes Daniel to the king, but only after trying to grab
some credit himself for finding an interpreter (v. 25).

"Well, do you have an answer for me?" asks Nebuchadnezzar (v. 26).

Again, Daniel refuses to reveal the interpretation without re-
vering the Interpreter.

Daniel answered before the king and said, "As for
the mystery about which the king has inquired, neither wise men, conjurers, magicians, nor diviners are
able to declare it to the king. However, there is a
God in heaven who reveals mysteries, and He has
made known to King Nebuchadnezzar what will take
place in the latter days. This was your dream and
the visions in your mind while on your bed. As for
you, O king, while on your bed your thoughts turned
to what would take place in the future; and He who
reveals mysteries had made known to you what will
take place. But as for me, this mystery has not been
revealed to me for any wisdom residing in me more
than in any other living man, but for the purpose
of making the interpretation known to the king,

and that you may understand the thoughts of your mind." (vv. 27–30)

"Let's set the record straight," says Daniel. "Not me, your advisors, nor any other human being can explain your dream, for one simple reason. It came from the God of heaven. He gave it, and only He can explain it to you. And He has chosen to do so through me."

What boldness! What humility! What an eternal perspective!

Concluding Thoughts

We'll analyze Nebuchadnezzar's dream in the next lesson. For now, let's stop here and glean some practical lessons from Daniel's example.

First, *God works best in humanly impossible predicaments.* Sometimes God allows us to be pushed to the edge of disaster, where there's no way out. Then He says, "Jump! I'll catch you." And He does. And we realize afresh that He can be trusted.

Second, *our most effective source of stability is prayer.* Not just because of whom we pray to but whom we pray with. God hears us, no matter if we're alone or in a group. But He provides comfort and encouragement by giving us friends who pray with us.

Third, *when God works, there's no room for pride, only praise.* Praise means recognizing who God is and what He has done. We've cheapened praise by reducing it to a religious mantra: "Praise the Lord, praise the Lord." Be specific. Give God the credit and glory for His *specific* blessings. Then we'll be less likely to take credit ourselves.

We serve a great God who can handle anything, work through anyone, and show Himself at any time. And that's no dream.

 Living Insights

Daniel's story is more than dreams and interpretations, it has practical lessons for God's people of all ages. What does Daniel 2:1–30 teach you about:

• Keeping God at the forefront of our thinking?

_____

_____

- Seeking Him when the pressure's on?

_____

_____

- Keeping a record of what God does for us?

_____

_____

- Knowing His Word?

_____

_____

- Consulting Him on decisions?

_____

_____

- Listening to God in a culture that would rather not hear from Him at all?

_____

_____

- Honoring Him when He works in our lives?

_____

_____

What, if anything, do you need to do to pay closer attention to the King of Kings?

_____

_____

_____

_____

Chapter 4

A BLUEPRINT OF TOMORROW

Daniel 2:31–49

A s for the mystery about which the king has inquired," we heard Daniel tell sleep-deprived Nebuchadnezzar in our previous chapter, "neither wise men, conjurers, magicians, nor diviners are able to declare it to the king. However, there is a God in heaven who reveals mysteries . . ." (Dan. 2:27–28a).

How typical of this man—to always be pointing to the God of heaven, no matter what the circumstance. Commentator Ronald Wallace makes note of this aspect of Daniel's faith and character.

> No doubt [Daniel] reacts to the situation around him differently from all the other religious men of Babylon because he alone is in touch with a God who cares and works practically and marvelously. . . .
>
> Throughout this situation, though he himself has seen no possible way open, Daniel has acted with complete confidence that God would give him, at the moment of need, wisdom to solve any problem, and strength to face up to any threat. He believed that, though he himself at the beginning saw no possible way through the dilemmas and complexities of the situation, yet all the time God had a way and a solution for everything; and surely God would make the way clear even at the moment of direst perplexity. He has been certain that in the crisis he and his friends would be able to pray as none of the others involved knew how, to a God who would never fail. He has gone about the task confident that he was to be an agent of a true miracle. Though he is weak and knows nothing, this man is nevertheless strong and knows everything because he is trusting the living God.[1]

Let's now see what it is that the Living God revealed to His servant.

---

1. Ronald S. Wallace, *The Message of Daniel: The Lord Is King*, The Bible Speaks Today Series (Downers Grove, Ill.: Inter-Varsity Press, n.d.), pp. 53–54.

Revelation of the Dream

In a clear and confident voice, Daniel unveils God's message to the king.

> "You, O king, were looking and behold, there was a single great statue; that statue, which was large and of extraordinary splendor, was standing in front of you, and its appearance was awesome." (Dan. 2:31)

In his mind's eye, Nebuchadnezzar once again sees the terrible statue towering over him, a halo of splendor emanating from its body. Daniel chooses a fitting word for the image: *awesome.*

> "The head of that statue was made of fine gold, its breast and its arms of silver, its belly and its thighs of bronze, its legs of iron, its feet partly of iron and partly of clay." (vv. 32–33)

The metals deteriorate in value from the head to the feet. As magnificent as it appears, the great colossus with a head of gold has feet of clay. The structure is entirely unstable and destined for a fall.

> "You continued looking until a stone was cut out without hands, and it struck the statue on its feet of iron and clay, and crushed them. Then the iron, the clay, the bronze, the silver and the gold were crushed all at the same time, and became like chaff from the summer threshing floors; and the wind carried them away so that not a trace of them was found. But the stone that struck the statue became a great mountain and filled the whole earth." (vv. 34–35)

Reminiscent of David's victory over Goliath, one stone brings down this giant. But, unexpectedly, the statue does not topple to the ground like a fallen tree. The impact of the stone pulverizes the entire structure. Nothing remains but dust, and that is blown away by the wind. In the place where the statue stood, the mysterious stone grows and grows, covering land and sea until it has taken over the whole earth.

As Nebuchadnezzar listens, his heart must quake with both wonder and terror—wonder that Daniel knows his dream, and terror as he relives it. What could it mean?

Interpretation of the Dream

Fortunately, God does not leave the dream's interpretation up to us. Through Daniel, He tells us what each part of the vision represents, beginning with the head of gold.

The Head of Gold: Babylonian Kingdom

> "You, O king, are the king of kings, to whom the God of heaven has given the kingdom, the power, the strength, and the glory; and wherever the sons of men dwell, or the beasts of the field, or the birds of the sky, He has given them into your hand and has caused you to rule over them all. You are the head of gold." (vv. 37–38)

The scepter of world power rests in Nebuchadnezzar's hand *because God placed it there* (see v. 21). God has set Nebuchadnezzar and his golden empire as the head of the world. But one day, God will supplant magnificent Babylon with another kingdom, the one symbolized by the silver chest and arms.

The Chest and Arms of Silver: Medo-Persian Kingdom

> "And after you there will arise another kingdom inferior to you." (v. 39a)

It must have been difficult for Nebuchadnezzar to believe an inferior kingdom could overthrow mighty Babylon. The first line of defense for the metropolis was a huge moat that tied into the Euphrates River—the main water source that ran through the center of the city. Also protecting Babylon were double walls that rose like stone cliffs into the sky. The ancient historian Herodotus measured them at about three hundred feet high and eighty-seven feet thick.[2] The defense systems were the most sophisticated in the world. Nebuchadnezzar clearly built Babylon to last.

In 539 B.C., however, the unthinkable happened. According to Herodotus, the combined forces of the Medes and the Persians diverted the Euphrates, causing the water level to drop and enabling

---

2. "Herodotus, who describes the city and walls some seventy years after the damage done by Xerxes in 478 B.C. . . . , appears to exaggerate the size." D. J. Wiseman, "Babylon," in *The International Standard Bible Encyclopedia*, rev. ed., ed. Geoffrey W. Bromiley (Grand Rapids, Mich.: William B. Eerdmans Publishing Co., 1979), vol. 1, p. 386. Even at half the size, though, the city defenses could resist the heaviest of assaults.

them to enter at night through the unguarded sluice gates. Great, golden Babylon fell without a fight or harm to the city, and in its place rose the Medo-Persian empire. Later, Darius the Mede required conquered nations to pay tribute in silver, which, interestingly, corresponds to the silver chest and arms.

The Belly and Thighs of Bronze: Grecian Kingdom

Daniel next tells Nebuchadnezzar that the bronze belly and thighs represent a government "which will rule over all the earth" (v. 39b). By 331 B.C., a young Greek named Alexander the Great had extended his rule as far as India, vanquishing the Persian empire. He "swept across the world of his day, conquering the known kingdoms of earth and weeping because he had no other worlds to conquer."[3] The Greek soldiers used shields made of bronze, hence the bronze in the image. Yet even Alexander's legacy would give way to the iron strength of another.

The Legs of Iron and Feet of Iron and Clay: Roman Kingdom

> "Then there will be a fourth kingdom as strong as iron; inasmuch as iron crushes and shatters all things, so, like iron that breaks in pieces, it will crush and break all these in pieces." (v. 40)

In 146 B.C., Roman legions like iron tanks rumbled across the Mediterranean world and eventually Europe, crushing everything in their path. But the wider the empire expanded, the more it deteriorated. External divisions did not cause the empire to crumble, though. Its true weakness came from within, as its iron-like assets mixed with its clay-like liabilities.

> "And in that you saw the feet and toes, partly of potter's clay and partly of iron, it will be a divided kingdom; but it will have in it the toughness of iron, inasmuch as you saw the iron mixed with common clay. And as the toes of the feet were partly of iron and partly of pottery, so some of the kingdom will be strong and part of it will be brittle. And in that you saw the iron mixed with common clay, they will

---

3. Ray C. Stedman, from the sermon transcript "The Last Act," given at Peninsula Bible Church, Palo Alto, California, February 2, 1969, p. 2. Copyright © 1969 RCS. All rights reserved.

combine with one another in the seed of men; but they will not adhere to one another, even as iron does not combine with pottery." (vv. 41–43)

This prophecy, though clearly foretelling the decline of the Roman Empire, goes far beyond that ancient age. Ray Stedman explains.

> The interesting thing now is that every single nation of this western hemisphere was begun by one of the nations of the Roman empire. Our entire Western world is Roman to the core. You can see that even in our own [U.S.] history. We have a senate which is one of the fundamental bases of our government, and which we copied directly from the Roman senate. The very republican form of the United States government is based upon the republic of Rome. Our courts, our laws, our military, all reflect the . . . forms of the Roman empire. . . . Now, what is the symbolism of [the iron mingled with clay]? . . . Iron symbolized an imperialistic attitude or form of government, the power and might of imperialism seeking to dominate and to rule by brute force and strength. Clay, on the other hand, is weak, pliable, easily molded. Most Bible scholars are right in identifying this as the principle of democracy. . . .
>
> The voice of the people is always a fickle voice. It is easily molded, like clay. That is what politicians capitalize on. . . . we are [also] subject to the tremendous pressures of mass media which play upon our minds to mold the will of the people. That is the weakness of democracy.
>
> . . . "they shall mingle together with the seed of men" . . . seems to imply a universal application, i.e., this is a grass roots matter; it permeates the masses. In the stream of humanity these two conflicting currents struggle together and as we near the end of this fourth kingdom it becomes a struggle at the grass roots level. Now it strikes me as highly significant that this is what we see arising in our own day. . . .
>
> What is happening in the nations of the West

in our day? Well, clearly they are torn by domestic strife. They are being weakened by internal conflict. There is enough iron yet to threaten with the power and strength of ancient Rome, but there is enough clay to weaken and paralyze so that nations are unable to accomplish their objectives. Thus we have the sight of great and powerful nations which are almost helpless to carry out what they set themselves to do. They are being throttled and thwarted by internal weakness, by struggles breaking out from within, by the unmixable principle of the voice of the people and the iron will of authority in conflict.[4]

The Stone That Became a Great Mountain: The Divine Kingdom

"And in the days of those kings the God of heaven will set up a kingdom which will never be destroyed, and that kingdom will not be left for another people; it will crush and put an end to all these kingdoms, but it will itself endure forever. Inasmuch as you saw that a stone was cut out of the mountain without hands and that it crushed the iron, the bronze, the clay, the silver, and the gold, the great God has made known to the king what will take place in the future; so the dream is true, and its interpretation is trustworthy." (vv. 44–45)

And so Daniel concludes God's message to the king.

As we examine this part of the prophetic scene, it's clear that the stone "cut out of the mountain without hands" is Jesus Christ (compare 1 Pet. 2:6–8). Its fantastic growth ties in with Isaiah's hopeful vision of the last days, when

The mountain of the house of the Lord
Will be established as the chief of the mountains,
And will be raised above the hills;
And all the nations will stream to it. (Isa. 2:2)

When will the Lord's mountain be established? When Christ returns. In an explosion of heavenly glory, He will shatter the

4. Stedman, "The Last Act," pp. 3, 4, 6.

foundations of every human institution and "set up a kingdom which will never be destroyed" (Dan. 2:44). Hallelujah!

Summary of Daniel's Interpretation

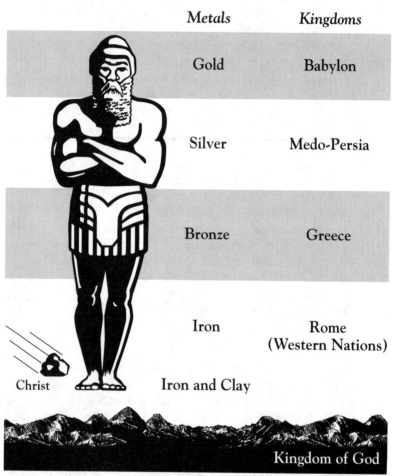

Metals	*Kingdoms*
Gold	Babylon
Silver	Medo-Persia
Bronze	Greece
Iron	Rome (Western Nations)
Iron and Clay	

Christ

Kingdom of God

The Promotion of the Prophet

Upon hearing the interpretation, Nebuchadnezzar's terror over his dream melts into fear of the Lord.

Then King Nebuchadnezzar fell on his face and

did homage to Daniel, and gave orders to present to him an offering and fragrant incense. The king answered Daniel and said, "Surely your God is a God of gods and a Lord of kings and a revealer of mysteries, since you have been able to reveal this mystery." (vv. 46–47)

Isn't it remarkable that when we accurately represent God, people will recognize Him? How pleased Daniel must have been to carry this pagan king's praises to the God of Israel.

The king then showers Daniel with "great gifts" and promotes him to "ruler over the whole province of Babylon and chief prefect over all the wise men of Babylon" (v. 48). The sudden rise to the top doesn't shake Daniel's humility, though. He honors his prayer partners by asking Nebuchadnezzar to appoint "Shadrach, Meshach and Abed-nego over the administration of the province of Babylon." And Daniel remains "at the king's court" as God's special light to the Gentiles (v. 49).

Application

Our journey through time via Nebuchadnezzar's dream leads us to two vital reminders for today. First, *we are rapidly approaching the end of time*. The governments of the world have been given the opportunity to use the iron of authority for good; but tragically, the clay of pride, deceit, and unfaithfulness destroyed their potential. We see society's foundation cracking more and more each day. The time is right for Christ to demolish the unsteady colossus we have created and start anew.

Second, *all investments in earthly kingdoms are temporary at best*. Our golden dreams may sparkle briefly in the sunlight, but eventually they all will come crashing down. Invest your life in what will last—the kingdom of God. Construct your future on Jesus the Rock. There is no firmer foundation.

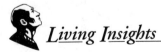 *Living Insights*

Nebuchadnezzar's gigantic statue symbolizes the four great empires of the ancient world; but in a broader sense, it represents something about all of us. Ronald Wallace explains:

It can stand for any system that tends to close itself to the living influence of the Spirit of Jesus Christ. It can tell us all plainly what lies in our future too, if we dare to stand in the way of the progress of the Word of God by which he rules. His kingdom is bound to gather momentum and grow in hidden force and power. All that cannot be taken up and incorporated into it will ultimately be shown up as vanity—as chaff that the wind blows away. We need not give only a political significance to this colossal statue. It can stand for our little empires, domestic, social, business, financial or ecclesiastical in the midst of which some of us sit enthroned, trying in vain to find security and satisfaction. It can stand merely for the image of our own future.[5]

Read Luke 12:16–21. What little empire did the rich man in Jesus' parable build? How was it scattered to the winds?

_____

_____

_____

In what do you find your security and satisfaction? Is it a little empire of your own making?

_____

_____

_____

How stable is it? Does it have feet of clay?

_____

_____

_____

If Christ were to return today, is there something in your life

5. Wallace, The Message of Daniel, p. 60.

34

that would be turned to dust?

_____

_____

_____

———◆———

Read Luke 12:29–34. In what does Jesus want us to find our security and satisfaction?

_____

_____

_____

In what ways can you build up your inheritance in Christ's kingdom?

_____

_____

_____

———◆———

Lord,
    Thank You for quietly stepping into the dreams of an ancient king and revealing his future. For in his destiny, I see my own. I see my face on the giant statue, and its form displays the gold, silver, bronze, and iron qualities of my life. Impressive, aren't I, Lord? But we both know about my feet of clay: my insecurities, my prideful moodiness, my greed.
    Thank You for the warning of the stone. When the colossus came crashing down, so did my life. When it turned to dust and the wind blew it away, I saw a glimpse of my future apart from You.
    Thank You for the promise of the mountain. The hope of something solid. Help me to set my foundation on this rock. To seek first Your kingdom. To live my life for Your glory. To surrender myself completely to You, my King eternal.

Chapter 5

A RAGTIME BAND AND A FIERY FURNACE

Daniel 3

Have you ever held firm to your convictions and done what is right only to have your problems heat up instead of cool down? It hurts, doesn't it? You may wonder, *I thought following Christ was supposed to take me to green pastures and quiet waters. What did I do to deserve this?*

Well, you've done nothing to deserve it, just as Job did nothing to deserve his pain and Jesus did nothing to deserve His. This kind of suffering is unjust—and the furnace of suffering is never hotter than when we suffer unjustly.

Yet the apostle Peter wrote that our response to this kind of pain can bring glory to our just and righteous God:

> For this finds favor, if for the sake of conscience toward God a man bears up under sorrows when suffering unjustly. For what credit is there if, when you sin and are harshly treated, you endure it with patience? But if when you do what is right and suffer for it you patiently endure it, this finds favor with God. (1 Pet. 2:19–20)

Why would patiently enduring wrong glorify God? Because it shows our trust in and the trustworthiness of "Him who judges righteously" (v. 23). By responding with endurance, we point to the greater reality of the righteous, omnipotent, sovereign Lord.

Need some help picturing this? Then turn to Daniel 3, where Daniel's friends Shadrach, Meshach, and Abed-nego wind up in a fiery furnace and a pagan king sees the glory of God.

The King's Image: A Statue

The fiery circumstances for the three Jews begin when Nebuchadnezzar builds an enormous statue.

Construction

Nebuchadnezzar the king made an image of gold,

the height of which was sixty cubits [90 feet] and its width six cubits [9 feet]; he set it up on the plain of Dura in the province of Babylon.[1] (v. 1)

The Septuagint, a Greek version of the Hebrew Old Testament, says that Nebuchadnezzar built the statue in the eighteenth year of his reign—sixteen years after Daniel's interpretation of the king's dream in chapter 2. In all that time, none of those prophecies have come true.[2] There's been no "silver" kingdom. No "bronze" kingdom. No "iron" kingdom. And certainly no sign of a magical flying stone.

So, pumped up with a renewed sense of invincibility, the king thumbs his nose at God and builds a massive idol as a glittering symbol of his sovereign rule.[3] The figure is every bit the colossus that he saw in his dream, except the entire image is overlaid in gold (not just the head)—and you can be sure the feet have not a trace of clay. No kingdom, natural or supernatural, is going to crush his statue . . . or his empire.

Instruction and Dedication

Having completed the monument, the king sends word

> to assemble the satraps, the prefects and the governors, the counselors, the treasurers, the judges, the magistrates and all the rulers of the provinces to come to the dedication of the image that Nebuchadnezzar the king had set up. (v. 2)

This assemblage of powerful people represents every ethnic group and religion under Nebuchadnezzar's authority. As the king surveys the colorful crowd milling around the base of the statue, the morning sun flashes brilliantly off the polished gold, practically blinding the eyes of the onlookers. When the moment is right, he signals for quiet, and the herald proclaims the royal decree:

---

1. The slender monument was about eight stories tall, or five times taller than Michelangelo's *David*, which is about eighteen feet high.

2. If the Septuagint is correct, the statue would have been built around the time Nebuchadnezzar conquered Jerusalem. Having presumably discredited the God of Israel, Nebuchadnezzar may have felt he had nothing to fear in erecting an image to the glory of Babylon.

3. Note how many times Nebuchadnezzar is referred to as "Nebuchadnezzar the king" in this chapter—seven times, and there are only nine such references in the whole book (the other two are in chapter 4). Clearly, a showdown is coming between this self-impressed, earthly king and the almighty King of Kings.

"To you the command is given, O peoples, nations and men of every language, that at the moment you hear the sound of the horn, flute, lyre, trigon, psaltery, bagpipe, and all kinds of music, you are to fall down and worship the golden image that Nebuchadnezzar the king has set up. But whoever does not fall down and worship shall immediately be cast into the midst of a furnace of blazing fire." (vv. 4–6)

What was Nebuchadnezzar's purpose in demanding this? Just to sate his arrogance? Commentator Dwight Pentecost shows us a more shrewd reason.

> The fact that the officials were commanded not only to fall down before the image, but also to worship it, indicates that the image had religious as well as political significance. Since no specific God is mentioned, it may be inferred that Nebuchadnezzar was not honoring one of the gods of Babylon, but rather was instituting a new form of religious worship with this image as the center. Nebuchadnezzar purposed to establish a unified government and also a unified religion. The king constituted himself as both head of state and head of religion. All who served under him were to recognize both his political and religious authority.[4]

Confronted by the king's command and within earshot of the roaring furnace, the government authorities bow down and pay homage to the statue when the orchestra begins to play (v. 7). However, while the throng of people touch their foreheads to the ground in worship, three Hebrews remain standing.

Accusation

Shadrach, Meshach, and Abed-nego, remember, hold influential positions "over the administration of the province of Babylon" (2:49). But a few spiteful and prejudiced Chaldeans (a class of astrologers and astronomers) notice their refusal to worship the

---

4. J. Dwight Pentecost, "Daniel," in *The Bible Knowledge Commentary*, Old Testament edition, ed. John F. Walvoord and Roy B. Zuck (Wheaton, Ill.: Scripture Press Publication, Victor Books, 1985), p. 1338.

king's idol and slink away to make their report. Notice how they embellish the facts to inflame the king's anger:

> "O king, live forever! You yourself, O king, have made a decree . . . . There are certain Jews whom you have appointed . . . [who] have disregarded you; they do not serve your gods or worship the golden image which you have set up." (3:9–12)

The charge rings out: Treason! By choosing to obey the Lord's command not to worship false gods (see Deut. 5:8–10), Shadrach, Meshach, and Abed-nego are about to face the test of their lives.

The Fiery Furnace: A Test

To Nebuchadnezzar, their refusal to worship the statue is a challenge to his supreme authority. Immediately, his anger flares up and he lashes out at the three Jews.

The King's Outrage

> Then Nebuchadnezzar in rage and anger gave orders to bring Shadrach, Meshach and Abed-nego; then these men were brought before the king. Nebuchadnezzar responded and said to them, "Is it true, Shadrach, Meshach and Abed-nego, that you do not serve my gods or worship the golden image that I have set up?" (Dan. 3:13–14)

As if he can't quite believe anyone would dare defy his orders, the king gives the trio one more chance to pledge their allegiance to the cultic image (v. 15a)—but not without reiterating the punishment if they don't:

> "But if you will not worship, you will immediately be cast into the midst of a furnace of blazing fire; and what god is there who can deliver you out of my hands?" (v. 15b)

What god is greater than Nebuchadnezzar? The king will soon find out.

The Hebrews' Faith

Despite the king's deadly threats, Shadrach, Meshach, and Abed-nego do not recant.

"O Nebuchadnezzar, we do not need to give you an answer concerning this. If it be so, our God whom we serve is able to deliver us from the furnace of blazing fire; and He will deliver us out of your hand, O king. But even if He does not,[5] let it be known to you, O king, that we are not going to serve your gods or worship the golden image that you have set up." (vv. 16–18)

They understand, as God's people throughout history have always known, that the battle is the Lord's (see 1 Sam. 17:47; 2 Chron. 20:14–15). They don't need to argue theology with the king and try to gain their own victory. Quiet resistance to the king's edict is all that's necessary.

Nebuchadnezzar may rule the world, but neither his glittering statue nor his great power can intimidate these three men or overpower the divine kingdom they represent.

The Furnace's Intensity

Enraged, Nebuchadnezzar orders the furnace made seven times hotter—as hot as the inferno blazing inside him (Dan. 3:19). Then he commands his strongest soldiers to bind the Hebrews and cast them into the white-hot furnace (v. 20). In the process, it is the king's soldiers who die from the flames (vv. 21–22), while Shadrach, Meshach, and Abed-nego disappear into the fire, still bound from head to toe (vv. 23).

For a moment, the king's ravenous anger is satisfied.

The Lord's Deliverance

Then Nebuchadnezzar the king was astounded and stood up in haste; he responded and said to his high officials, "Was it not three men we cast bound into the midst of the fire?" They answered and said to the king, "Certainly, O king." He answered and said, "Look! I see four men loosed and walking about in the midst of the fire without harm, and the appearance of the fourth is like a son of the gods!" Then Nebuchadnezzar came near to the door of the

---

5. True faith does not presume that God will always make things go our way. True faith obeys God first and leaves the outcome up to Him.

40

furnace of blazing fire; he responded and said, "Shadrach, Meshach and Abed-nego, come out, you servants of the Most High God, and come here!" Then Shadrach, Meshach and Abed-nego came out of the midst of the fire. And the satraps, the prefects, the governors and the king's high officials gathered around and saw in regard to these men that the fire had no effect on the bodies of these men nor was the hair of their head singed, nor were their trousers damaged, nor had the smell of fire even come upon them. (vv. 24–27)

What god can deliver His people out of Nebuchadnezzar's hands? The Most High God, the only true God, the God of Daniel, Shadrach, Meshach, and Abed-nego. Truly, Nebuchadnezzar was experiencing the power of the stone from his dream—the kingdom of God that would one day crush all man-made empires.

Nebuchadnezzar's statue seems to have lost its luster, hasn't it? What began as a monument to his supremacy has become a reminder of his subordinate status to a King greater than himself. And to his credit, he is the first to admit it.

The King's Response

Nebuchadnezzar responded and said, "Blessed be the God of Shadrach, Meshach and Abed-nego, who has sent His angel and delivered His servants who put their trust in Him, violating the king's command, and yielded up their bodies so as not to serve or worship any god except their own God. Therefore, I make a decree that any people, nation or tongue that speaks anything offensive against the God of Shadrach, Meshach and Abed-nego shall be torn limb from limb and their houses reduced to a rubbish heap, inasmuch as there is no other god who is able to deliver in this way." Then the king caused Shadrach, Meshach and Abed-nego to prosper in the province of Babylon. (vv. 28–30)

Isn't it ironic? The mighty king who ordered the world to bow before his image now bows before the King of the world.

The Lessons Learned: An Application

God chose to rescue Shadrach, Meshach, and Abed-nego, but His plan for us may be different. If you're in a furnace of suffering because of standing for your faith, the following three principles will help you endure the heat with patience.

First, keep in mind that *God is sovereign, whether the result of your obedience is triumph or tragedy.* When things go well for us, it's easy to acknowledge God's sovereignty. But when the bottom drops out, we often wonder, "Is God still in control?"

The fact is, God would still have been in control had He allowed Shadrach, Meshach, and Abed-nego to die in the flames—as He allowed thousands of martyrs throughout history to die. He may deliver; He may not. Our part is to trust His character and His sovereign plan, whatever it may be, and to obey.

Second, don't forget that *suffering is necessary, whether it seems fair or not.* Pain has its positive side—which is always easier to see when we're not suffering. Did you notice that the only thing the fire burned were the cords that bound Shadrach, Meshach, and Abed-nego? Often, suffering burns away those things that bind us, that keep us from serving and following God completely. The goal, as Peter put it, is that

> the proof of your faith, being more precious than
> gold which is perishable, even though tested by fire,
> may be found to result in praise and glory and honor
> at the revelation of Jesus Christ. (1 Pet. 1:7)

The third thing to remember is, *deliverance is impressive, whether it is witnessed by the godly or the ungodly.* What really dazzled the people on the plain of Dura that day wasn't the gold on the statue but the golden faith that Shadrach, Meshach, and Abed-nego displayed as a result of their fiery ordeal. When we come out of our furnace experiences stronger and freed up from the things that once bound us, we are a living testimony to God's presence and power. And that's impressive to those who are watching.

Even more than impressive, it can be life-changing.

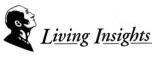 *Living Insights*

It wasn't the blazing furnace that forced the government officials to bend their knees to the pagan idol. It was their *fear* of the fire. When fear grips us, it can bend our knees too. It can hold us back. It can paralyze us. We dare not speak, for fear of ridicule. We dare not act, for fear of pain. We dare not live, for fear of dying.

There is a power far greater than fear, though. Can you guess what it is? A measure of it exists deep within each of us, and all we must do is draw from it to increase its liberating strength. What is that dynamic force? Faith.

By faith, Shadrach, Meshach, and Abed-nego "quenched the power of fire" (Heb. 11:34). Their faith in God didn't literally extinguish the flames. It doused the *power* of the flames: the fear of death.

Does a certain fear have a grip on you? What is it?

_____

_____

_____

Imagine your fear as a fiery furnace. What's it like to look into it and feel its heat? Describe the power this fear has over you.

_____

_____

_____

Fear is one of the main forces that can keep us from obeying Christ fully. What one thing would you like to do for the Lord that your fear prevents you from doing?

_____

_____

_____

What was Shadrach's, Meshach's, and Abed-nego's attitude toward God in Daniel 3:16–18? How can their example help you overcome your fear?

The trusting trio could pass through the flames because they knew that, whatever happened, God was waiting for them on the other side. Do you need a little more convincing that this promise holds true for you too? Then meditate on the following assurances from God, and let Him begin to free you from fear's binding hold.

Deuteronomy 31:6–8   Luke 12:6–7
Proverbs 3:25–26   Romans 8:35–39
Isaiah 41:10   1 Peter 3:14–16
Isaiah 43:1–2

———◆———

No coward soul is mine,
No trembler in the world's storm-troubled sphere:
I see heaven's glories shine,
And faith shines equal, arming me from fear.[6]

6. Emily Brontë, as quoted in *Women's Wisdom through the Ages: Timeless Quotations on Life and Faith,* comp. Mary Horner and Vinita Hampton Wright (Wheaton, Ill.: Harold Shaw Publishers, 1994), p. 8.

Chapter 6

INSOMNIA, INSANITY, AND INSIGHT
Daniel 4

To Nebuchadnezzar, gods were a dime a dozen. Every nation's gods had their particular flavors—different names, different looks, but essentially, they were all the same. With the right religious exercise, you could tame them into giving you what you wanted or, at the least, leaving you alone. As we've seen in our study, however, the king had never encountered a god like the God of Israel. There was something unique about Him—something terrifyingly real.

Nebuchadnezzar didn't seem to know what to do with this God who kept stepping into his life at the most unpropitious moments. He admired God's power, yet he couldn't bring himself to submit his life. For a man who had conquered vast armies, surrender didn't come easy.

But surrender did come eventually, when the proud king who controlled the world finally gave control of his life to God.

The King and His Dream

As we open Daniel 4, we notice that Nebuchadnezzar himself is writing this portion of Daniel's book.

> Nebuchadnezzar the king to all the peoples, nations, and men of every language that live in all the earth: "May your peace abound!" (v. 1)

Every chapter so far in this book has begun with Nebuchadnezzar the king. (Daniel 5 and 6 will also begin with the rulers of that time: Belshazzar and Darius.) Why this emphasis on earthly kings, and especially Nebuchadnezzar?

Remember, at the time, the power and grandeur of Nebuchadnezzar's Babylon was unparalleled in the world. His was the greatest kingdom, and he was the greatest king. This king had even overpowered God's people, which many undoubtedly equated with the overpowering of the Jews' God.

Daniel, however, knew differently. He knew that God was still in charge: He mandated His people's captivity as a discipline for

45

their idolatry and sin, and Nebuchadnezzar was the tool He used to accomplish this. One of Daniel's themes throughout his book, then, is that God is the Most High God and greater than any earthly king. Or as Daniel put it:

> "Let the name of God be blessed forever and ever,
> For wisdom and power belong to Him.
> And it is He who changes the times and the epochs;
> He removes kings and establishes kings." (2:20–21a)

That's why it is so significant in Daniel 4 that the mightiest king who had ever lived comes to realize that there is One far greater than him. In fact, Nebuchadnezzar is so moved by God's glory and power that before he relates how he came to know this God personally, he bursts forth with praise.

A Declaration of Praise

Nearing the end of his renowned forty-three-year reign, when most kings would be fanning the feathers of their own accomplishments, Nebuchadnezzar puts the works of the Lord on display.[1]

> "It has seemed good to me to declare the signs and
> wonders which the Most High God has done for me.
> How great are His signs,
> And how mighty are His wonders!
> His kingdom is an everlasting kingdom,
> And His dominion is from generation to
> generation." (vv. 2–3)

Nebuchadnezzar, who has customarily been saluted with, "O king, live forever!" (2:4; 3:9), now praises the only King who can *really* live forever!

What happened in the king's life to make him go from boasting in himself to boasting in the Lord? Turning the calendar back eight years, he tells that it all began with a dream.

---

1. Nebuchadnezzar's reign lasted from 605–562 B.C. The events described in this chapter probably took place about 570 B.C., thirty years after the fiery furnace incident. See J. Dwight Pentecost, "Daniel," in *The Bible Knowledge Commentary*, Old Testament edition, ed. John F. Walvoord and Roy B. Zuck (Wheaton, Ill.: Scripture Press, Victor Books, 1985), p. 1341.

A Description of His Dream

> "I, Nebuchadnezzar, was at ease in my house and
> flourishing in my palace. I saw a dream and it made
> me fearful; and these fantasies as I lay on my bed and
> the visions in my mind kept alarming me." (4:4–5)

With the empire secure and the royal treasury bursting, these
were the golden years of his monarchy. Yet, instead of settling back
in an easy chair of opulence, the king was sitting on pins and
needles. What could this dream mean?

As with his earlier dream, he summoned his wise men to guide
him to some answers. But just as before, they could offer no help
(vv. 6–7). Finally, Daniel entered the confusion.

> "Daniel came in before me, whose name is Belte-
> shazzar according to the name of my god, and in
> whom is a spirit of the holy gods; and I related the
> dream to him, saying, 'O Belteshazzar, chief of the
> magicians, since I know that a spirit of the holy gods
> is in you and no mystery baffles you, tell me the
> visions of my dream which I have seen, along with
> its interpretation.'" (vv. 8–9)

Because the king hadn't yet given his life to the Lord, his
perspective was still pagan. He called Daniel Belteshazzar, after his
god, Bel. And he considered Daniel a magician of the gods instead
of a prophet of the Most High God.

With Daniel listening intently, Nebuchadnezzar revealed his
dream:

> "'Now these were the visions in my mind as I lay
> on my bed: I was looking, and behold, there was a tree
> in the midst of the earth, and its height was great.
> The tree grew large and became strong,
> And its height reached to the sky,
> And it was visible to the end of the whole
> earth.
> Its foliage was beautiful and its fruit abundant,
> And in it was food for all.
> The beasts of the field found shade under it,
> And the birds of the sky dwelt in its branches,
> And all living creatures fed themselves from it.

I was looking in the visions in my mind as I lay on my bed, and behold, an angelic watcher, a holy one, descended from heaven. He shouted out and spoke as follows:

"Chop down the tree and cut off its branches,
Strip off its foliage and scatter its fruit;
Let the beasts flee from under it,
And the birds from its branches.
Yet leave the stump with its roots in the
     ground,
But with a band of iron and bronze around it
In the new grass of the field;
And let him be drenched with the dew of
     heaven,[2]
And let him share with the beasts in the grass
of the earth.
Let his mind be changed from that of a man,
And let a beast's mind be given to him,
And let seven periods of time pass over him.
This sentence is by the decree of the angelic
     watchers,
And the decision is a command of the holy
     ones,
In order that the living may know
That the Most High is ruler over the realm
     of mankind,
And bestows it on whom He wishes,
And sets over it the lowliest of men.""

(vv. 10–17)

The Prophet and His Response

When the king finished, a dark feeling of dread welled up in Daniel so that he couldn't speak. Verse 19 says that he "was appalled for a while as his thoughts alarmed him."

Seeing the trepidation in Daniel's eyes, Nebuchadnezzar encouraged him to speak: "Belteshazzar, do not let the dream or its interpretation alarm you" (v. 19b). Then the king braced himself for Daniel's explanation.

2. At this point, the pronoun referring to the stump changes from *it* to *him*—providing us a clue to the meaning of the dream.

Interpretation

Like a doctor who must bear tragic news to an ill friend, Daniel first let the king know how he wished it wasn't so:

> "'My lord, if only the dream applied to those who hate you, and its interpretation to your adversaries!'" (v. 19c)

Then he slowly unveiled the dream's meaning. The luxuriant tree represented the king, whose branches of influence had spread far and wide, prospering all the nations with the fruit of his magnificent reign. His majesty stretched to the skies like the mighty cedars of Lebanon and his "dominion to the end of the earth" (v. 22).

But Daniel trembled at the thought of what would happen next:

> "'This is the interpretation, O king, and this is the decree of the Most High, which has come upon my lord the king: that you be driven away from mankind, and your dwelling place be with the beasts of the field, and you be given grass to eat like cattle and be drenched with the dew of heaven; and seven periods of time will pass over you, until you recognize that the Most High is ruler over the realm of mankind, and bestows it on whomever He wishes.'" (vv. 24–25)

For seven years, a mental illness would reduce Nebuchadnezzar from emperor to animal. Why? So he would "recognize that the Most High is ruler over the realm of mankind, and bestows it on whomever He wishes" (see also vv. 17, 32). This is Daniel's theme, not only for this chapter but also for his whole book.

It is the Lord Almighty who raises kings, and it is the Lord who brings them down. And sometimes, in His grace, He raises them again, as Daniel shows Nebuchadnezzar:

> "'And in that it was commanded to leave the stump with the roots of the tree, your kingdom will be assured to you after you recognize that it is Heaven that rules.'" (v. 26)

Confrontation

At this point, the easiest thing for Daniel to do would have been to walk away before God's judgment struck. But he cared enough for Nebuchadnezzar to confront him:

>"'Therefore, O king, may my advice be pleasing to you: break away now from your sins by doing righteousness, and from your iniquities by showing mercy to the poor, in case there may be a prolonging of your prosperity.'" (v. 27)

Daniel's confrontation grew out of the soft soil of a long-term relationship with the king. Notice the wise principles he followed:

- he approached him with tact
- he was specific and honest
- he gave the king hope

Daniel did what he could; the rest was up to the king. Only time would tell how Nebuchadnezzar would respond.[3]

The Lord and His Dealings

Patiently, the Lord waited for the dream and Daniel's advice to take root. But as the weeks passed and the fearful impact of the dream faded, the king's heart swelled with pride.

Misery of Insanity

>"Twelve months later he was walking on the roof of the royal palace of Babylon. The king reflected and said, 'Is this not Babylon the great, which I myself have built as a royal residence by the might of my power and for the glory of my majesty?' While the word was in the king's mouth, a voice came from heaven, saying, 'King Nebuchadnezzar, to you it is declared: sovereignty has been removed from you.'" (vv. 29–31)

It was time for the Lord to pull the royal rug out from under this haughty king. "Immediately," verse 33 says, "the word concerning Nebuchadnezzar was fulfilled." Nebuchadnezzar's mind snapped and

>"he was driven away from mankind and began eating grass like cattle, and his body was drenched with the dew of heaven, until his hair had grown like eagles'

---

3. For further study on healthy confrontation, see David Augsburger's book *Caring Enough to Confront*, rev. ed. (Ventura, Calif.: Gospel Light Publications, Regal Books, 1980).

feathers and his nails like birds' claws."[4] (v. 33)

What a pitiful scene of human degradation. Nebuchadnezzar had been "treated with a severe mercy," as C. S. Lewis put it.[5] It was *severe*, for God had to cut down everything precious in his life, even his mind. But it was a *mercy*, for out of the severed stump grew the tender green shoot of salvation.

Declarations of Praise

When his trial ended, Nebuchadnezzar finally submitted to God, the King of Kings.

> "But at the end of that period I, Nebuchadnezzar, raised my eyes toward heaven, and my reason returned to me, and I blessed the Most High and praised and honored Him who lives forever;
> For His dominion is an everlasting dominion,
> And His kingdom endures from generation
>   to generation.
> And all the inhabitants of the earth are
>   accounted as nothing,
> But He does according to His will in the host
>   of heaven
> And among the inhabitants of earth;
> And no one can ward off His hand
> Or say to Him, 'What hast Thou done?'"
> (vv. 34–35)

The story ends with Nebuchadnezzar receiving back his sovereignty with an even greater measure of majesty and splendor than before (v. 36). But this time, the king gives *all* the glory to God.

> "Now I Nebuchadnezzar praise, exalt, and honor the King of heaven, for all His works are true and His ways just, and He is able to humble those who walk in pride." (v. 37)

---

4. Nebuchadnezzar's dementia sounds like *zoanthropy*, which is "a form of mental disorder in which the patient imagines himself to be a beast." *Webster's New Universal Unabridged Dictionary*, 2d ed., see "zoanthropy."

5. From a letter by C. S. Lewis to Sheldon Vanauken, in *A Severe Mercy*, by Sheldon Vanauken (New York, N.Y.: Harper and Row, Publishers, Bantam Books, 1977), p. 211.

The Account and Its Application

At least two golden truths shine from the crucible of Nebuchadnezzar's experience. First, *God's judgment may be slow, but it is certain.* We sometimes think His silence means He's asleep or doesn't care, but nothing could be further from the truth. God always tries the slow and gentle approach first, loving us and waiting for us to submit to His will. He gave Nebuchadnezzar a dream, a fiery miracle, another dream, and a whole year to humble himself. God's patience is geared toward our repentance (see also Rom. 2:4; 2 Pet. 3:9). His patience, however, does set limits.

Second, *God will go to extremes to show us that He's Lord.* Sometimes, like a surgeon, God has to hurt us to heal us. He uses affliction like a scalpel, cutting deep into the cancerous core of our sin. We cry as if the world will end, but out of our pain comes new life. Eventually, we are glad that God cared enough to discipline us and, through the doorway of sorrow, give us a second chance.

 Living Insights

The proverb cautions us: "Pride goes before destruction, And a haughty spirit before stumbling" (Prov. 16:18). That's what God through Daniel was trying to tell Nebuchadnezzar, but the king was too dazzled by his own reflection to see he was heading toward a fall.

Suppose Daniel was standing before you. What prideful attitudes would God have him point out to you? Stubbornness? Conceit? Having all the answers? Self-centeredness? In what shape or size does pride come in your life?

In relation to your spouse: _____

Your ex-husband or -wife:_____

Your children: _____

A coworker:_____

A relative: _____

A friend: _____

Are you heading toward a fall? Do you have relationships that are crumbling, resentments that are building barriers? What consequences do you see on the horizon if you don't deal with your pride?

_____

_____

_____

Nebuchadnezzar learned humility the hard way. What truths did he discover that helped him overcome his pride (see Dan. 4:1–3, 34–37)?

_____

_____

_____

How can his lesson help you keep your heart from swelling with pride?

_____

_____

_____

_____

_____

_____

_____

_____

_____

_____

_____

_____

_____

Chapter 7

THE HANDWRITING ON THE WALL

Daniel 5

The last words of Nebuchadnezzar the Bible records are words of praise to the Lord, "Now I Nebuchadnezzar praise, exalt, and honor the King of heaven, for all His works are true and His ways just" (Dan. 4:37a). He doesn't stop there, though. His final thought concerns a lesson he learned the painful way: "He is able to humble those who walk in pride" (v. 37b).

When we come to chapter 5, we meet a new king, Belshazzar, Nebuchadnezzar's grandson. Unfortunately, Belshazzar has received none of the benefits of Nebuchadnezzar's hard-learned spiritual truths. About the only trait he has picked up is his grandfather's discarded pride—without a trace of the heart that was finally responsive to God.

A Setting to Understand

Let's take a moment to see how one generation's revival became the future generations' rebellion. The following chart shows Nebuchadnezzar's family and the line of kings that led up to Belshazzar.

Nebuchadnezzar's Family Tree[1]

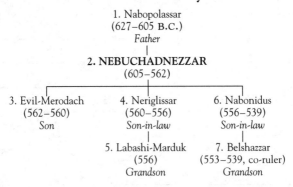

1. Nabopolassar
(627–605 B.C.)
Father

2. NEBUCHADNEZZAR
(605–562)

3. Evil-Merodach	4. Neriglissar	6. Nabonidus
(562–560)	(560–556)	(556–539)
Son	*Son-in-law*	*Son-in-law*
	5. Labashi-Marduk	7. Belshazzar
	(556)	(553–539, co-ruler)
	Grandson	*Grandson*

1. Adapted from the chart, "Kings of the Neo-Babylonian Empire," by J. Dwight Pentecost, "Daniel," in *The Bible Knowledge Commentary*, Old Testament edition, ed. John F. Walvoord and Roy B. Zuck (Wheaton, Ill.: Scripture Press, Victor Books, 1985), p. 1326.

After Nebuchadnezzar's death, it didn't take long for the dry rot of greed and ambition to eat away the branches of royal family tree. His son, Evil-Merodach, reigned only two years before his power-hungry brother-in-law, General Neriglissar, assassinated him and stole the crown. After a six-year reign, Neriglissar died, and his young son, Labashi-Marduk, stepped into power. His rule, though, lasted only a few months before he was murdered in a coup led by Nabonidus.[2]

Nabonidus spent most of his reign away from Babylon, securing the borders and strengthening the empire. He appointed his son, Belshazzar, as co-ruler and left him in charge of Babylon.

In the heavily fortified city, Belshazzar lounged comfortably on his velvet-covered throne. No invader had been able to storm the city for over a thousand years.[3] Babylon was considered impregnable.

That was about to change.

The Medo-Persian Military

In the distance, the Medo-Persian king Cyrus and his army were galloping southward toward Babylon. Seeing the growing threat, Nabonidus and his troops headed them off at Opis on the Tigris River. A great battle ensued, and Nabonidus was forced to withdraw, leaving Cyrus an open road to Babylon.

Safe within the city, Belshazzar made light of the news. What harm could Cyrus' spears and arrows do against Babylon's massive stone walls and impassable moat? When Cyrus besieged the city, Belshazzar still just shrugged his shoulders. There was a twenty-year supply of food in the huge granaries. Cyrus and his men would run out of provisions long before Belshazzar and his people.

So the arrogant king scoffed at Cyrus' siege and conceived the perfect way to show how confident of victory he was—he threw a party. Let's pick up the story with the festivities already in progress.

A Feast to Remember

> Belshazzar the king held a great feast for a thou-
> sand of his nobles, and he was drinking wine in the

---

2. Historians disagree as to whether Nabonidus murdered Neriglissar or his son. If he dethroned Neriglissar, Nabonidus would have assumed the throne in 560 or 559 B.C.

3. See Gleason L. Archer, Jr., "Daniel," in *The Expositor's Bible Commentary*, gen. ed. Frank E. Gaebelein (Grand Rapids, Mich.: Zondervan Publishing House, Regency Reference Library, 1985), vol. 7, pp. 69–70.

presence of the thousand. (Dan. 5:1)

His head spinning from the wine, Belshazzar feels a euphoric sense of invincibility welling up within him. He is the greatest king of the world! Greater than Cyrus! Greater than Nebuchadnezzar! Greater than God Himself! In his drunken bravado, he performs a brazen act of blasphemy that no other Babylonian king before him dared to do.

Belshazzar's Blasphemy

> When Belshazzar tasted the wine, he gave orders to bring the gold and silver vessels which Nebuchadnezzar his father had taken out of the temple which was in Jerusalem,[4] in order that the king and his nobles, his wives, and his concubines might drink from them. . . . They drank the wine and praised the gods of gold and silver, of bronze, iron, wood, and stone. (vv. 2, 4)

Nebuchadnezzar had stored Israel's temple vessels, showing respect for their value as sacred treasures. By using them to toast his own gods, Belshazzar shows his contempt for both his grandfather and the God he grew to worship.

Unlike the inanimate idols, however, who respond to praise and desecration in pretty much the same way—dumb as a rock—the true God doesn't tolerate such mockery.

God's Hand of Judgment

> Suddenly the fingers of a man's hand emerged and began writing opposite the lampstand on the plaster of the wall of the king's palace, and the king saw the back of the hand that did the writing. Then the king's face grew pale, and his thoughts alarmed him; and his hip joints went slack, and his knees began knocking together. (Dan. 5:5–6)

Belshazzar must realize deep down that the message spells judgment. Sobered up, the king calls in the experts, "the conjurers, the Chaldeans and the diviners," and promises that the one who can

---

4. Nebuchadnezzar, of course, was not Belshazzar's father in a literal sense. *Father* here and throughout the passage can be translated *forefather*.

interpret the inscription "will be clothed with purple, and have a necklace of gold around his neck, and have authority as third ruler in the kingdom" (v. 7).[5]

But just as in the days of Nebuchadnezzar, God's message confounds the Babylonian wise men (v. 8; see also 2:2–10; 4:6–7). Seeing their helplessness, Belshazzar grows more alarmed and turns more pale with fright (5:9).

The queen (probably Belshazzar's grandmother, Nebuchadnezzar's surviving wife) is the only one in the court who thinks to summon Daniel (v. 10). Brushing the dust off the past, the queen mother recalls him.

> "There is a man in your kingdom in whom is a spirit of the holy gods; and in the days of your father, illumination, insight, and wisdom like the wisdom of the gods were found in him. And King Nebuchadnezzar, your father, your father the king, appointed him chief of the magicians, conjurers, Chaldeans, and diviners. This was because an extraordinary spirit, knowledge and insight, interpretation of dreams, explanation of enigmas, and solving of difficult problems were found in this Daniel, whom the king named Belteshazzar. Let Daniel now be summoned, and he will declare the interpretation." (vv. 11–12)

A Man to Admire

How many years has it been since Daniel has been called by a king? Now in his eighties, he still carries himself with a steadiness born out of a lifetime of faith in God. Before the sapling king, he stands like an oak tree—his character firmly rooted, his integrity unshakable.

Yet the disdainful Belshazzar sees Daniel as only "one of the exiles from Judah, whom my father the king brought from Judah" (v. 13). Looking down his royal nose, he offers Daniel the same deal: riches and power for an interpretation (v. 16). Daniel, however, can't be bought:

> Then Daniel answered and said before the king,

5. Nabonidus and Belshazzar were the first and second rulers. The wise interpreter would be third, directly under them.

"Keep your gifts for yourself, or give your rewards to someone else; however, I will read the inscription to the king and make the interpretation known to him." (v. 17)

Before he unveils the meaning, Daniel gives the self-indulgent monarch a lesson from history.

Reviewing the Past

"O king, the Most High God granted sovereignty, grandeur, glory, and majesty to Nebuchadnezzar your father. And because of the grandeur which He bestowed on him, all the peoples, nations, and men of every language feared and trembled before him; whomever he wished he killed, and whomever he wished he spared alive; and whomever he wished he elevated, and whomever he wished he humbled." (vv. 18–19)

Squarely confronting Belshazzar's attempted condescension in verse 13, Daniel reminds the king that all the power Nebuchadnezzar ever had—even to take God's people into captivity—came from God. That lesson was a hard one for Nebuchadnezzar to learn too.

"But when his heart was lifted up and his spirit became so proud that he behaved arrogantly, he was deposed from his royal throne, and his glory was taken away from him. He was also driven away from mankind, and his heart was made like that of beasts, and his dwelling place was with the wild donkeys. He was given grass to eat like cattle, and his body was drenched with the dew of heaven, until he recognized that the Most High God is ruler over the realm of mankind, and that He sets over it whomever He wishes." (vv. 20–21)

That last line repeats the familiar theme from chapter 4 (see vv. 17, 25, 32). All crowns of authority belong to the Lord, who gives them and takes them away with the same sovereign hand. Not even kings have a right to boast before God.

Reading the Charges

Having built his case from the past, Daniel confronts Belshazzar with the charges against him:

> "Yet you, his son, Belshazzar, have not humbled your heart, *even though you knew all this.*" (5:22, emphasis added)

The guilt weighs even heavier on Belshazzar's shoulders because he knows the truth about God through his grandfather's experience. Yet that knowledge has done nothing to change his life.

> "But you have exalted yourself against the Lord of heaven; and they have brought the vessels of His house before you, and you and your nobles, your wives and your concubines have been drinking wine from them; and you have praised the gods of silver and gold, of bronze, iron, wood and stone, which do not see, hear or understand. But the God in whose hand are your life-breath and your ways, you have not glorified." (v. 23)

How foolish for Belshazzar to worship lifeless objects instead of the One who holds his life in His hand. Now that hand is about to take from him everything in which he boasted: his throne, his kingdom, and his life.

Revealing the Verdict

Daniel reads the inscription like a jury foreman announcing the verdict:

> "Now this is the inscription that was written out: 'MENĒ, MENĒ, TEKĒL, UPHARSIN.'" (v. 25)

Literally, the translation is "a mina, a mina, a shekel, and half-shekels" (NASB margin note). To interpret this cryptic message, Daniel digs down to the lexical roots. *Menē* comes from the verb "to number, to reckon"; *tekēl*, from the verb "to weigh"; and *upharsin*, from the verb "to break in two, to divide."[6]

> "This is the interpretation of the message: 'MENĒ'— God has numbered your kingdom and put an end to it. 'TEKĒL'—you have been weighed on the scales and found deficient. 'PERĒS'—your kingdom

---

6. Pentecost, "Daniel," p. 1346.

has been divided and given over to the Medes and Persians." (vv. 26–28)

Belshazzar listens but, amazingly, seems unmoved by the devastating prediction. He orders that Daniel be given the purple robe and the golden necklace, and he elevates him to the third ruler of the kingdom—as if the kingdom would just keep going (v. 29). Doesn't he realize the party's over?

Unknown to the king, Cyrus' ingenious commander, Ugbaru, has diverted the Euphrates River, lowering the level of the water running through Babylon. That same night, the Medo-Persian troops waded in under the river gates, took the city by surprise, and "Belshazzar the Chaldean king was slain" (v. 30).

A Message to Apply

As we step out of the fading pageantry of ancient Babylon, we'll find that we can take at least two lessons back to our own world.

First, *God's judgment may seem slow, but it is thorough.* By A.D. 200, the once-mighty Babylon, with its towering walls and beautiful gardens, was completely deserted[7] (compare Jer. 27:4–5; chaps. 50–51; Isa. 13:17–22). Today it isn't even a whistle-stop along the Baghdad railroad. We don't need to wonder if God will do something about the evil that goes on in this world (see Hab. 1:1–4). He long ago saw its beginning and determined its end.

And second, *never underestimate the power of one solitary, godly life.* Against the bleak backdrop of judgment stood one reassuring and constant light: Daniel. He endured because he courageously spoke God's truth and refused to compromise his character. Are we doing the same? Our life may be the only light some people will ever see.

 Living Insights

Taking serious things lightly was Belshazzar's deadly mistake. When the strong winds of war started whipping around the walls of Babylon, instead of boarding up windows and bracing himself, he threw a hurricane party. What attitude do you think was at the

---

7. See *The International Standard Bible Encyclopedia*, rev. ed., gen. ed. Geoffrey W. Bromiley (1979; reprint, Grand Rapids, Mich.: William B. Eerdmans Publishing Co., 1988), vol. 1, p. 390.

heart of Belshazzar's actions (see Prov. 21:24)?

_____

_____

We might not throw a party during a hurricane warning, but we might ignore other danger signals in our lives—a persistent pain in our body, a red light blinking in our conscience, the sober advice of an older "Daniel."

Are you taking lightly a serious situation? If so, what is it?

_____

_____

What attitude is at the heart of your actions?

_____

_____

What new course do you need to set to avoid disaster?

_____

_____

Belshazzar's cavalier attitude also expressed itself in his disregard for God. Instead of fearing the Lord, he toyed with Him. He treated the Lion of Judah like a tamed pussycat. What lesson do you learn about fearing the Lord from Belshazzar's negative example?

_____

_____

Don't let pride blur your ability to see what you should be taking seriously in life. Belshazzar's story calls out a warning to all who are wise enough to listen.

Chapter 8

THE MARKS OF INTEGRITY
Daniel 6:1–16a

In Daniel 6, we come to one of the most familiar of all the Bible's stories—Daniel in the lions' den. Can't you almost see those flannelgraph images you cut your spiritual teeth on in Sunday school? This favorite story, though, has a lot more to it than we saw in our childhood flannel figures. Commentator Ronald Wallace capsulizes this chapter's message:

> empires rise and kings come and go, fashions and life-styles change, but the one stable thing in the midst of all this change is Daniel himself—the man of God who does justice, and loves kindness, and walks humbly with his God [Mic. 6:8].[1]

Does Daniel's stability remind you of Jesus' words?

> "Therefore, everyone who hears these words of Mine, and acts upon them, may be compared to a wise man, who built his house upon the rock. And the rain descended, and the floods came, and the winds blew, and burst against that house; and yet it did not fall, for it had been founded upon the rock." (Matt. 7:24–25)

The soundness, the integrity of our faith and character is what will keep us standing in the midst of life's storms—just as it did for Daniel. Let's join our old friend in chapter 6 of his book and discover how the marks of his integrity can mark our lives as well.

Some Introductory Matters

With the death of Belshazzar and the accession of Darius the Mede (Dan. 5:30–31), we pass from the gold head of Nebuchadnezzar's statue to its silver chest and arms (2:31–32, 39). The sunset of Babylon's kingdom has now become the dawning of the Medo-Persian empire.

---

1. Ronald S. Wallace, *The Message of Daniel: The Lord Is King,* The Bible Speaks Today Series (Downers Grove, Ill.: InterVarsity Press, n.d.), p. 118.

What would this new power look like? How would the Medes and Persians organize their reign?[2]

Political Situation of Darius the King

Unlike the Babylonian kings, who were absolute monarchs, the new rulers liked to delegate responsibilities.

> It seemed good to Darius to appoint 120 satraps over the kingdom, that they should be in charge of the whole kingdom. (6:1)

The word *satrap* comes from an Old Persian word that meant "protector of the kingdom," or more specifically a "provincial governor."[3] Can you imagine trying to oversee 120 governors? One person couldn't possibly keep track of them all—which is just what corrupt politicians would count on. Realizing this, Darius appointed

> over them three commissioners (of whom Daniel was one), that these satraps might be accountable to them, and that the king might not suffer loss. (v. 2)

Once "ruler over the whole province of Babylon and chief prefect over all the wise men" (2:48), Daniel—by this time an octogenarian—is now a commissioner in Medo-Persia. It's not hard to guess what kind of leader Daniel was.

Personal Life of Daniel the Prophet

> Then this Daniel began distinguishing himself among the commissioners and satraps because he possessed an extraordinary spirit.[4] (6:3a)

What comprised this "extraordinary spirit"? Certainly his gifts from God: the "knowledge and intelligence in every branch of

---

2. Darius the Mede is not to be confused with the later Persian emperor Darius I (the Great). Possibilities for the identity of Daniel's Darius include (1) another name for Cyrus, (2) someone Cyrus appointed to rule Babylon while Cyrus ruled the greater Persian empire, (3) Cyrus' governor Gubaru (a.k.a. Ugbaru or Gobyras), who conquered Babylon while Belshazzar feasted, or (4) Cyrus' son Cambyses. See J. Dwight Pentecost, "Daniel," in *The Bible Knowledge Commentary*, Old Testament edition, ed. John F. Walvoord and Roy B. Zuck (Wheaton, Ill.: Scripture Press, Victor Books, 1985), p. 1347.

3. *The New Bible Dictionary*, 2d ed. (1982; reprint, Downers Grove, Ill.: InterVarsity Press, 1991), see "satrap."

4. This isn't the first time Daniel has been picked out of the crowd because of his spirit (see 4:8, 9, 18; 5:11, 12, 14).

literature and wisdom" and his ability to understand visions and dreams (1:17; see also 5:11–12). But between the lines, in Daniel's tactful, respectful, and reasonable approach to people and situations, we can find another facet: an excellent attitude (1:8–13; 2:14–16, 27–28; 4:19, 27).

First Mark of Integrity: An Excellent Attitude

Daniel knew that the Lord was sovereign over all appointments and disappointments (Ps. 75:7). And because he was secure in his God, Daniel was secure in himself. This competent, positive, and cooperative attitude of Daniel's caught the king's eye, and he "planned to appoint him over the entire kingdom" (Dan. 6:3b).

Not everyone, however, was as secure as Daniel.

Plot against Daniel

Horrified that some old exile from a conquered country, a Hebrew no less, would be promoted above all of them, the bigoted satraps and commissioners got together to get rid of their enemy.

Attempted Accusations

> Then the commissioners and satraps began trying to find a ground of accusation against Daniel in regard to government affairs; but they could find no ground of accusation or evidence of corruption, inasmuch as he was faithful. (v. 4a)

Daniel's enemies trailed him, looking for some payola, a conflict of interest, a hint of incompetence, a numbers racket—anything! But they couldn't find a speck of dirt on this guy, because he was faithful in his work.

Second Mark of Integrity: Faithful in Work

How rare to find someone who is absolutely trustworthy in their employment (see Prov. 20:6–7). Daniel was such a man, and not only on the job but also in his personal life.

> No negligence or corruption was to be found in him. (Dan. 6:4b)

Third Mark of Integrity: Personal Purity

Daniel's honesty remained solid and sure. He tolerated no trace of hypocrisy; he had nothing to hide. He lived his life knowing there was a God to whom he was accountable. Focused on that true God, he grew like Him in godliness.

His persecutors, however, were not impressed with his righteousness; instead, it put them off. They remained undeterred in their scheme, and quickly devised another tack.

> Then these men said, "We shall not find any ground of accusation against this Daniel unless we find it against him with regard to the law of his God." (v. 5)

Written Injunction

With the specifics of their plan in hand, they skulked in to see the king.

> "King Darius, live forever! All the commissioners of the kingdom, the prefects and the satraps, the high officials and the governors have consulted together that the king should establish a statute and enforce an injunction that anyone who makes a petition to any god or man besides you, O king, for thirty days, shall be cast into the lions' den. Now, O king, establish the injunction and sign the document so that it may not be changed, according to the law of the Medes and Persians, which may not be revoked." Therefore King Darius signed the document, that is, the injunction. (vv. 6b–9)

Did you notice the lie they started with: "*All* the commissioners . . ."? All but one! And what an approach: bald-faced flattery. What king of that day wouldn't have liked to rule the religious realm as well as the political? Playing right into their manipulative hands, Darius could barely see beyond his puffed-up ego to sign the injunction.

Public Arrest

With his fate sealed, what was Daniel to do?

> Now when Daniel knew that the document was signed, he entered his house (now in his roof chamber he had windows open toward Jerusalem); and he continued kneeling on his knees three times a day, praying and giving thanks before his God, as he had been doing previously. (v. 10)

Ronald Wallace notes, "The orientation of his prayer-closet windows was a symbol of the continual tendency of his mind and thought, when not immersed in Babylon itself, to turn towards . . . Yahweh."[5] Note that he didn't bang open his windows to flaunt his prayer life and get everybody's attention. He already had them open toward Jerusalem.

Also, Daniel didn't suddenly seek God in a moment's panic. His walk with Him was consistent—"as he had been doing previously." He was accustomed to bringing all his needs before his Lord, trusting Him to keep His Word. And that trust shielded him from fear's grip, so that he could continue "praying and *giving thanks* before his God."[6]

Fourth Mark of Integrity: A Consistent Walk with God

Only a consistent walk with God could see him through what would happen next.

> Then these men came by agreement and found Daniel making petition and supplication before his God. (v. 11)

Ah-ha! The scoundrel—he was praying! They had their evidence now. Having burst in on Daniel mid-prayer, they hightailed it to the king. What a sweet victory for them. Not only did they get to destroy Daniel, they also got to watch his friend the king writhe under the sharp point of his own self-glorifying law.

> Then they approached and spoke before the king about the king's injunction, "Did you not sign an injunction that any man who makes a petition to any god or man besides you, O king, for thirty days, is to be cast into the lions' den?" The king answered and said, "The statement is true, according to the law of the Medes and Persians, which may not be revoked." Then they answered and spoke before the king, "Daniel, who is one of the exiles from Judah, pays

---

5. Wallace, *The Message of Daniel*, p. 106.

6. We can gather several tips for a consistent prayer life from Daniel's example. First, he had a set place where he met regularly with God. Second, he had made prayer a habit—three times every day. Third, he had a prayer position—kneeling. And fourth, he had a heart for God that didn't fail when the outlook got dark.

no attention to you, O king, or to the injunction which you signed, but keeps making his petition three times a day." Then, as soon as the king heard this statement, he was deeply distressed and set his mind on delivering Daniel; and even until sunset he kept exerting himself to rescue him. (vv. 12–14)

Darius sought to be worshipped as a god. But only the true God could rescue Daniel now.

Then these men came by agreement to the king and said to the king, "Recognize, O king, that it is a law of the Medes and Persians that no injunction or statute which the king establishes may be changed."

Then the king gave orders, and Daniel was brought in and cast into the lions' den. (vv. 15–16a)

You'll have to wait for our next chapter to see how the story ends!

Some Practical Lessons

So far in this familiar story, we can learn three practical lessons that apply to us as well as Daniel. First, *you will seldom get what you deserve from people, so don't expect it.* When we genuinely deserve honor, our value will seldom be noticed. And when we genuinely deserve criticism, we'll seldom get the confrontation we need. The best thing to do, then, is to seek affirmation from the Lord (see Col. 3:23–24).

Second, *you will always get what is best from God—don't doubt it.* God's best may not look like what we expect or come when we think we need it. But we mustn't doubt His care or His character while we're enduring the pain of waiting (see Matt. 7:9–11).

And last, *your ability to handle both people's worst and God's best is directly related to the consistency of your walk.* Remember, when Daniel was cast into the lions' den, he didn't know how the story would turn out. Yet he was at peace. Devoured or delivered, he was going to keep his trust in God, because no matter the outcome, his God was trustworthy.

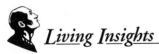 *Living Insights*

What, do you suppose, engraved the marks of integrity on Daniel's character and life? One of the clues might be found in

Daniel 6:10. What do you find there?

_____

That's right—faithful, consistent, disciplined prayer. Through prayer, Daniel continually aligned his life with God, which proved to be the wellspring of his godly character.

How consistent is your prayer life?

Are you satisfied with it? If so, that's great! You might want to think about using your experience to teach and encourage others.

If you are not satisfied though, you've got nowhere to go but up (pun intended)! Let's begin right now to turn your inconsistency into an opportunity for growth.

For the next two weeks, including Sundays, set aside ten minutes in the morning and ten at night to

1. express worship to God by praising Him for His marvelous attributes,

2. confess your sins and your sorrow for them,

3. thank God for who He is, especially relating to what's happening in your life,

4. bring your concerns for others before Him,

5. ask for specific help or guidance you might need.[7]

With just this short amount of time spent looking into the face of God, how can you help but begin to reflect His image?

To help you get started and stick with your plan, we've provided the following calendar so you can check off each morning and evening that you pray. By learning to invest your time and effort in this way, you'll be on your way to a beautiful lifetime habit—with a beautiful life to show for it.

	SUN	MON	TUES	WED	THUR	FRI	SAT
A.M.							
P.M.							
A.M.							
P.M.							

7. For further study on prayer, see chapter 13, "True Confessions."

Chapter 9

THE LIONS IN DANIEL'S DEN

Daniel 6:16b–28

So far in Daniel 6 we have seen Daniel serve King Darius with faithful excellence and Darius plan to promote Daniel. We have also seen the other commissioners and satraps jealously plot Daniel's demise and trick the king into signing an injunction against his friend and loyal assistant. The upshot of all this? Innocent Daniel has wound up in a lions' den.[1]

How unjust!

Why didn't God prevent this? Isn't He a shield for His people, protecting them from becoming victims of evil? Doesn't His Word promise, "For it is Thou who dost bless the righteous man, O Lord, Thou dost surround him with favor as with a shield" (Ps. 5:12)?

How can we reconcile what has happened to Daniel (and Job and Jesus and the prophets and apostles and all the martyrs throughout history) with these confident words from the Psalms?

Perhaps it would help to recall the purpose of a shield. A shield isn't needed in a time of peace but in a time of war. A shield, then, doesn't exempt us from battle; rather, it equips us for it. From this fact alone we can come to understand that we will be in the midst of the fray, but God will fight right beside us.

Also, because we are such time-bound creatures with little sense of eternity, we get caught up in wanting our deliverance *now*. God's help, though, has His ultimate time frame in view, along with our ultimate good: the infinite well-being of our souls. Jesus had this view in mind when He prayed,

> "I have given them Thy word; and the world has hated them, because they are not of the world, even as I am not of the world. I do not ask Thee to take them out of the world, but to keep them from the evil one." (John 17:14–15; see also 14:18–27)

We may be in the Evil One's world; but if we belong to God, we are never in the Evil One's hand.

---

1. Interestingly, in a Bible that flatters none of its heroes, not one sin is recorded about Daniel. Of course, being human, he did sin. But his deep commitment to following God and His ways is what he is remembered for.

The apostle Peter also suffered injustice for doing right by God (see Acts 4:1–3; 5:17–18, 25–41; 12:1–6). Let's turn again to his first letter, which offers some insightful parallels to Daniel's story.

Peter's Perspective

Perhaps Peter had Daniel's example in mind when he wrote:

> Submit yourselves for the Lord's sake to every human institution, whether to a king as the one in authority, or to governors as sent by him for the punishment of evildoers and the praise of those who do right. (1 Pet. 2:13–14)

And when Daniel's enemies could find "no ground of accusation or evidence of corruption" in him (Dan. 6:4), Daniel modeled Peter's next assertion:

> For such is the will of God that by doing right you may silence the ignorance of foolish men. (1 Pet. 2:15)

The only way his enemies could defeat Daniel was to call his righteousness unrighteous, sort of like calling purple, orange. With his integrity suddenly made illegal by the signed injunction, Daniel illustrated Peter's counsel to face unfairness with a quiet trust in God.

> If when you do what is right and suffer for it you patiently endure it, this finds favor with God. (v. 20b, see also vv. 18–19)

Remember why this pleases God? Not because He finds injustice in any way tolerable or expects His children to be the doormats of the world. But because our patient endurance points to the trustworthiness of our just God (v. 23). It also helps us get out of the way so God can go to work (see Rom. 12:19, 21).

And would God ever go to work for Daniel! Let's return to Daniel 6 and see how the King of Kings dealt with the king of beasts.

Daniel's Deliverance

"Many are the afflictions of the righteous," Scripture tells us honestly, but it also encourages us that "the Lord delivers him out of them all" (Ps. 34:19). What could be more afflicting than getting tossed into a pit full of big, hungry lions?

Maybe standing on the outside, helplessly . . . like Darius.

Anxious Moments

Having explored any and every possible way to save Daniel, the king had no choice but to follow the letter of the law (Dan. 6:14–15).

> Then the king gave orders, and Daniel was brought in and cast into the lions' den. The king spoke and said to Daniel, "Your God whom you constantly serve will Himself deliver you." (v. 16)

That's quite an extraordinary statement from a pagan king who had recently decided he could be a god too. Darius and Daniel must have developed a friendship that was open enough for Daniel to talk about his God with the king. And Darius might have thought, if such a sensible man as Daniel was willing to risk his life for this God, then perhaps He could come through for Daniel after all.

> And a stone was brought and laid over the mouth of the den; and the king sealed it with his own signet ring and with the signet rings of his nobles, so that nothing might be changed in regard to Daniel. (v. 17)

What might a lions' den have looked like? Commentator C. F. Keil describes similar dens found in Morocco as being large, square, subterranean caverns divided by a center wall with a door in it to transfer the animals to either side for feeding and cleaning. The cavern had two openings: one above that was ringed by a short wall and remained open to let in fresh air, and the mouth and entrance on the side that was covered by a large, flat stone.[2] J. Dwight Pentecost adds that "the seal, an impression made in clay by an image on a ring, would inform others that the stone was not to be tampered with in an effort to free Daniel."[3]

With the seal set,

> the king went off to his palace and spent the night fasting, and no entertainment was brought before him; and his sleep fled from him. (v. 18)

---

2. C. F. Keil, *Biblical Commentary on the Book of Daniel*, trans. M. G. Easton (Grand Rapids, Mich.: William B. Eerdmans Publishing Co., 1959), p. 216.

3. J. Dwight Pentecost, "Daniel," in *The Bible Knowledge Commentary*, Old Testament edition, ed. John F. Walvoord and Roy B. Zuck (Wheaton, Ill.: Scripture Press, Victor Books, 1985), p. 1349. Does this remind you of another seal on another rock (see Matt. 27:62–66)?

Torn apart by worry, guilt, and anguish, King Darius passed a tormented night. He clearly cared for Daniel and could hardly wait for morning.

Blessed Relief

> Then the king arose with the dawn, at the break of day, and went in haste to the lions' den. And when he had come near the den to Daniel, he cried out with a troubled voice. The king spoke and said to Daniel, "Daniel, servant of the living God, has your God, whom you constantly serve, been able to deliver you from the lions?" (vv. 19–20)

Barely waiting for the first rays of sunrise, Darius rushed to the den, hoping he wouldn't find what he feared. What he found was a miracle.

> Then Daniel spoke to the king, "O king, live forever! My God sent His angel and shut the lions' mouths, and they have not harmed me, inasmuch as I was found innocent before Him; and also toward you, O king, I have committed no crime." (vv. 21–22)

Divinely vindicated, Daniel didn't even mind conversing with the king while still in the den! And immensely pleased, the king soon removed Daniel to lion-free land, where

> no injury whatever was found on him, because he had trusted in his God. (v. 23b)

There's the banner over Daniel's life—"He had trusted in his God."

Furious Vengeance

If you believe "hell hath no fury like a woman scorned," you ought to see a never-to-be-duped-again king!

> The king then gave orders, and they brought those men who had maliciously accused Daniel, and they cast them, their children, and their wives into the lions' den; and they had not reached the bottom of the den before the lions overpowered them and crushed all their bones. (v. 24)

Looks like this ruins the theory that the lions didn't eat Daniel because they weren't hungry! Rather, it confirms the truth that God's judgment on those who oppose His people and ways is sure.

Glorious Praise

Reminiscent of Nebuchadnezzar's response to God, Darius, too, felt compelled to proclaim His glories as far as he possibly could.

> Then Darius the king wrote to all the peoples, nations, and men of every language who were living in all the land: "May your peace abound! I make a decree that in all the dominion of my kingdom men are to fear and tremble before the God of Daniel;
> For He is the living God and enduring forever, And His kingdom is one which will not be destroyed,
> And His dominion will be forever.
> He delivers and rescues and performs signs and wonders
> In heaven and on earth,
> Who has also delivered Daniel from the power of the lions." (vv. 25–27)

Like the exultant peals of cathedral bells, so rings out this theme of Daniel: The Living God is King, and His indestructible kingdom will last forever! He cares for those who trust in Him—so don't lose hope!

Happy Ending

With Daniel rescued, God glorified, the king happy, and the enemies vanquished, we close with this happy postscript:

> So this Daniel enjoyed success in the reign of Darius and in the reign of Cyrus the Persian. (v. 28)

Solomon once wrote, "An arrogant man stirs up strife, But he who trusts in the Lord will prosper" (Prov. 28:25). We've certainly seen this come true in Daniel's life, haven't we?

But Daniel's prosperity wasn't limited to his political success. He prospered because through his obedience and trust, God's glory shone forth and saved a pagan king (see Matt. 5:16).

Hmm. Now there's a worthy goal for patiently enduring unjust suffering—bringing a lost soul to eternal life . . . showing a fellow struggler that there is One who "delivers and rescues and performs signs and wonders In heaven and on earth" (Dan. 6:27).

Daniel's calling is our calling too, if we'll listen to it above the lions' roar.

 ## Living Insights

Shh. I don't know if you've noticed, but there are lions in your den. That one over there is mauling your checkbook, while her cubs have reduced your savings to shreds. Oh, and that one on the sofa's got a couple of your relationships—you'd never think cat's play could be so cruel. And old Clarence stretched out by the fireplace, he's got one paw on what's left of your health while the rest is digesting.

Why on earth is this happening? You were walking along with God, often courageously so, and all of a sudden you're being eaten alive by painful and undeserved circumstances.

Sometimes in Scripture these lions go by another name: *trials.* They usually entail some combination of people going sideways on us and God wanting us to grow in response. That brings to mind still another name: *pain.* Trials hurt, don't they?

But if we try to avoid the pain, running from it or pretending it away, how do we show that God is real, that He is life, that He is trustworthy? How can we show those in darkness how to find the Light? How do we testify that life is a more valid option than death?

When you're suffering, what is your goal—besides relief, which is perfectly normal (see Rev. 21:4)? Take some time to think through your deepest values; then write down the things you would like your suffering to show. And remember, you are not doing this alone (see Ps. 46:1).

_____

_____

_____

_____

_____

_____

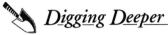 *Digging Deeper*

In finishing Daniel 6, we have come to the halfway point in the book of Daniel. The first six chapters have underscored God's sovereignty through historical events, while the next six will highlight that same theme through Daniel's prophetic dreams and visions of the future. Before we venture into the challenging mysteries of chapters 7–12, let's review the foundation Daniel has laid for us in chapters 1–6.

CHAPTER 1: How is God's superiority over Nebuchadnezzar shown in chapter 1? (Clue: See especially verses 15 and 19.)

_____

_____

_____

CHAPTER 2: The theme of Daniel is explicitly established in Daniel's prayer of thanks after God reveals to him Nebuchadnezzar's dream and its interpretation. Which verses state that theme?

_____

_____

_____

Recalling Nebuchadnezzar's dream of the statue, name the materials and empires that correspond to the body's parts.

Body Parts	Metal/Material	Empire
Head		
Chest and Arms		
Belly and Thighs		
Legs, Feet, Toes		

What destroyed the statue, and what did it symbolize?

_____

_____

_____

CHAPTER 3: Why is Nebuchadnezzar's question at the end of verse 15 the pivotal point of this chapter? How is it answered?

_____

_____

_____

CHAPTER 4: Why is this chapter the climax of all the stories about Nebuchadnezzar? (Clue: Reread verses 3b, 17, 25, 34–37.)

_____

_____

_____

CHAPTER 5: Why did God deal more harshly with Belshazzar than with Nebuchadnezzar? (Clue: Reread verses 17–23.)

_____

_____

_____

CHAPTER 6: How does Daniel show the Lord's sovereignty in this chapter?

_____

_____

_____

Chapter 10

A PROPHETIC COLLAGE
Daniel 7

As we cross the threshold into the last half of the book of Daniel, we move from history to prophecy, from the literal to the symbolic. Like Salvador Dalí's paintings in the 1930s, the images in these chapters are liquid and dreamlike, even nightmarish in their abstraction. We feel as if we're stepping into another world where natural laws do not apply. Everything seems surrealistic . . . visionary . . . puzzling.

Putting the pieces together is difficult, mainly because all the pieces aren't here. Daniel himself has trouble making sense of the collage of images. That's because the divine Artist who planted them in his mind designed them to be obscure. God isn't giving us a full-blown picture of the future, only fragments and portions, just enough to reassure us that He's in control and to inspire us to stay true, no matter what the future may hold.

Overview of Daniel 7

We can examine the prophetic collage in Daniel 7 from three angles. *Chronologically*, the chapter takes us back in time to a dream Daniel had fourteen years prior to Belshazzar's final feast and the handwriting on the wall (chap. 5).

> In the first year of Belshazzar king of Babylon Daniel saw a dream and visions in his mind as he lay on his bed; then he wrote the dream down and related the following summary of it. (Dan. 7:1)

Daniel would have been around sixty-eight years old at this time, having faithfully served Babylon for most of his life. Belshazzar was new on the throne, the empire was well in hand, and the Medo-Persian storm wasn't even visible on the horizon. Yet, in spite of the calm political breezes, Daniel saw a stormy vision from the Lord about the days to come. All was not as well as it seemed.

Viewing Daniel 7 *structurally*, we notice that the chapter divides neatly into two parts: Daniel's vision in verses 1–14 and the interpretation in verses 15–28. Key phrases to look for are "I was looking" and "I kept looking" (vv. 2, 4, 6, 7, 9, 11, 13, 21). To further clarify the structure, we see that

- verses 2–8 reveal the four beasts,
- verses 9–12 show the judgment from the Ancient of Days,
- verses 13–14 unveil the triumphant coming of the Son of Man,
- verses 15–27 give the explanation of it all.

Finally, we can look at the chapter *comparatively*. Daniel's dream ties in closely with Nebuchadnezzar's dream of the statue in Daniel 2. The following chart brings these two prophetic passages together.

Daniel 2 *The Statue*	Daniel 7 *The Animals*	*The Kingdoms*
Golden head	Winged lion	Babylon
Silver chest and arms	Lopsided bear	Medo-Persia
Bronze belly and thighs	Four-headed leopard	Greece
Legs of iron/feet of iron and clay	Terrible beast	Rome (Western nations)

The Vision Revealed

Having briefly overviewed the passage, let's now follow Daniel as he ushers us into the strange world of his dream.

Elements and Animals

> Daniel said, "I was looking in my vision by night, and behold, the four winds of heaven were stirring up the great sea." (Dan. 7:2)

Right from the beginning, his dream pulsates with symbolism. Commentator W. A. Criswell writes,

> The sea is shaken to its depths by the four raging winds of heaven. The numeral four in apocalyptic literature is the numeral representing the world. The four winds of the heavens, the four seasons, the four corners of the compass, all represent the whole earth. . . . The raging sea, so distressed and convulsed, is a picture of social revolution and the passions of humanity. Daniel sees humanity as a great

sea that is shaken from its center to its circumference, from its height to its depth. It is the turbulent, tumultuous sea of human life.[1]

Out of the divinely supervised chaos of world events arise four beasts, "coming up from the sea, different from one another" (v. 3). Let's take a look at each of the animals Daniel saw.

The lion. Verse 4 shows the first beast.

> "The first was like a lion and had the wings of an eagle. I kept looking until its wings were plucked, and it was lifted up from the ground and made to stand on two feet like a man; a human mind also was given to it."

Human mind comes from the word *lēbāb*, which means "heart, understanding, mind."[2] This was the only beast that had any vestige of human emotion, conscience, or moral will.

The bear. Then comes another beast,

> "a second one, resembling a bear. And it was raised up on one side, and three ribs were in its mouth between its teeth; and thus they said to it, 'Arise, devour much meat!'" (v. 5)

Commentator J. Dwight Pentecost observes that "this command suggests that kingdoms operate by divine appointment, not their own authority. In devouring other kingdoms . . . the bear was fulfilling God's purpose."[3]

The leopard. The third strange animal Daniel sees is

> "like a leopard, which had on its back four wings of a bird; the beast also had four heads, and dominion was given to it." (v. 6)

---

1. W. A. Criswell, *Expository Sermons on the Book of Daniel* (Grand Rapids, Mich.: Zondervan Publishing House, 1972), vol. 4, p. 25. Another option for identifying the "four winds of heaven" is provided by J. Dwight Pentecost: "The word translated 'winds' may also be rendered 'spirits,' that is, angels. Elsewhere in Scripture this word is used to refer to God's providential actions in the affairs of men through angels" (see Ps. 104:4; Heb. 1:7). "Daniel," in *The Bible Knowledge Commentary*, Old Testament edition, ed. John F. Walvoord and Roy B. Zuck (Wheaton, Ill.: Scripture Press, Victor Books, 1985), p. 1350.

2. *Theological Wordbook of the Old Testament,* ed. R. Laird Harris, Gleason L. Archer, Jr., Bruce K. Waltke (Chicago, Ill.: Moody Press, 1980), vol. 1, p. 466.

3. Pentecost, "Daniel," p. 1350.

Note again God's control: "dominion was *given* to it."
The terrible beast. His last vision is the worst of all:

> "After this I kept looking in the night visions, and
> behold, a fourth beast, dreadful and terrifying and
> extremely strong; and it had large iron teeth. It de-
> voured and crushed, and trampled down the remain-
> der with its feet; and it was different from all the beasts
> that were before it, and it had ten horns." (v. 7)

Ronald Wallace picks up the terror these beasts must have
evoked in Daniel.

> Instead of seeing, as before, the succession of coming
> world empires as four deteriorating parts in a mag-
> nificent but unstable colossus, he saw them as a series
> of four filthy and cruel *beasts*, arising out of, and
> belonging to, the wild slimy *sea* of this world's tur-
> bulent life (verse 3) . . . lusting only with an in-
> satiable desire to spread cruelty and further chaos,
> each preying on its predecessor, and existing mainly
> to fight and devour. As the whole fearful drama was
> played out before his eyes his horror mounted, for
> each succeeding beast became more cruel and more
> monster-like than its predecessor. The face of hu-
> manity was blotted out in the struggle.[4]

Terrifying as the fourth beast is, Daniel can't stop staring at it—
particularly at the ten horns on its hideous head. As he gazes at them,
something bizarre happens. They begin to take on lives of their own!

> "While I was contemplating the horns, behold, an-
> other horn, a little one, came up among them, and
> three of the first horns were pulled out by the roots
> before it; and behold, this horn possessed eyes like
> the eyes of a man,[5] and a mouth uttering great
> boasts." (v. 8)

---

4. Ronald S. Wallace, *The Message of Daniel: The Lord Is King,* The Bible Speaks Today
Series (Downers Grove, Ill.: InterVarsity Press, n.d.), pp. 120–21.

5. The "eyes like the eyes of a man" denote this horn's intelligence. See Pentecost, "Daniel,"
p. 1351. Note the contrast between the first beast, which was ennobled with a human mind/
heart, and this little horn, which used its superior human intellect for arrogance and blasphemy.

With the shrill, prideful self-praise of the little horn still ringing in his ears, Daniel suddenly sees a new scene bright with true holiness—and judgment.

Thrones and Judgment

> "I kept looking
> Until thrones were set up,
> And the Ancient of Days took His seat;
> His vesture was like white snow,
> And the hair of His head like pure wool.
> His throne was ablaze with flames,
> Its wheels were a burning fire.
> A river of fire was flowing
> And coming out from before Him;
> Thousands upon thousands were attending Him,
> And myriads upon myriads were standing before
>   Him;
> The court sat,
> And the books were opened." (vv. 9–10)

Everything about the scene suggests judgment—God taking His seat, the river of fire flowing like lava from His throne, the heavenly witnesses, the books opening. "It is a terrifying thing to fall into the hands of the living God," especially when that God "is a consuming fire" (Heb. 10:31; 12:29). The only one who doesn't have enough sense to grasp this, despite his intellect, is the little horn, whose blasphemies rise to heaven.

> "Then I kept looking because of the sound of the boastful words which the horn was speaking; I kept looking until the beast was slain, and its body was destroyed and given to the burning fire." (Dan. 7:11)

When the smoke clears, the horn is finally quiet and the terrible beast is dead. How does God deal with the other three animals?

> "As for the rest of the beasts, their dominion was taken away, but an extension of life was granted to them for an appointed period of time." (v. 12)

So all the beasts are either destroyed or removed from power. Then Daniel looks again and sees a final figure enter the scene, emerging not from the tumultuous sea but from the brilliant sky.

Intervention

> "I kept looking in the night visions,
> And behold, with the clouds of heaven
> One like a Son of Man was coming,
> And He came up to the Ancient of Days
> And was presented before Him.
> And to Him was given dominion,
> Glory and a kingdom,
> That all the peoples, nations, and men of every
>   language
> Might serve Him.
> His dominion is an everlasting dominion
> Which will not pass away;
> And His kingdom is one
> Which will not be destroyed."[6] (vv. 13–14)

The coronation of the Son of Man, Jesus Christ, marks the dawn of a new day in the earth—the kingdom of God. This is the day of worldwide redemption, peace, and justice that God's people throughout time have longed to see (see Isa. 11:1–10; Mic. 4:1–8; Zeph. 3:14–20; Phil. 2:9–11).

With the crown of the kingdom resting gloriously on Christ's head, God's prophetic collage is finished. Daniel, however, has just begun sorting out the imagery.

Interpretation

Distressed by what he has seen, the prophet approaches "one of those who [are] standing by" (probably an angel) and begins "asking him the exact meaning of all this" (Dan. 7:16). Here is the interpretation given to Daniel.

> "'These great beasts, which are four in number, are four kings who will arise from the earth. But the saints of the Highest One will receive the kingdom and possess the kingdom forever, for all ages to come.'" (vv. 17–18)

The angel ties the vision together with a message of hope: despite the terrors in the world, God still sits on the throne, and His people will win in the end.

---

6. Here again is Daniel's glorious theme (see also Dan. 2:44; 4:3, 34b; 6:26b).

What kings or kingdoms do the beasts symbolize? The *lion* with eagle's wings that was made to stand like a man represents Nebuchadnezzar and the Babylonian kingdom.[7] Like the lion's wings, Nebuchadnezzar's pride was "plucked" when he went insane for seven years. After he was humbled, God raised him up and made him greater than before (see 4:31–37)—perhaps because he had gained a heart of compassion (compare 4:27).

The *bear* pictures the Medo-Persian empire. Where one side of the bear was raised up higher than the other, so the power in the empire was uneven. The Medes initiated the kingdom, but the Persians came to dominate and eventually absorb them into their culture. The three ribs in the bear's mouth could represent the three kingdoms preceding this empire: Egypt, Assyria, and Babylon; or they could symbolize the three regions conquered by the Persians: Babylon, Lydia, and Egypt.[8]

The *leopard* symbolizes the Greek empire. A leopard is quick and vicious, but imagine the swiftness of a leopard with wings. With such amazing speed, Alexander the Great conquered the world. The four heads represent Alexander's four generals who divvied up his empire when he died.

The *terrible beast* is harder to figure out. In 7:19–22, Daniel presses for an explanation of the fourth beast and its ten horns, especially concerned because the little horn "was waging war with the saints and overpowering them" (v. 21). The angel responds:

> "'The fourth beast will be a fourth kingdom on the
> earth, which will be different from all the other
> kingdoms, and it will devour the whole earth and
> tread it down and crush it.'" (v. 23)

In one sense, the beast represents the Roman empire, with its powerful legions that devoured the world with iron-teethed ferocity. But in a broader sense, it symbolizes Rome's descendants: today's Western nations. The angel explains that "out of this kingdom ten kings will arise" (v. 24a). In other words, from the pool of Western nations, ten national leaders will join forces in a coalition of power. They will form a confederacy of states perhaps similar to the

---

7. "The lion and eagle were both symbols of Babylon" (see Jer. 4:5–13; Ezek. 17:1–21). Pentecost, "Daniel," p. 1350.

8. See Pentecost, "Daniel," p. 1350.

Common Market in Europe, also known as the European Economic Community (EEC).[9]

The angel continues:

> "'Another [king] will arise after them, and he will be different from the previous ones and will subdue three kings.'" (v. 24b)

To gain control, this boastful new leader (the "little horn") will force three of the ten national leaders out of power. In verses 25–26, the angel gives five particulars about this world dictator, whom the New Testament reveals as the Antichrist (in the next chapter, we'll examine Revelation 13 for more details about the Antichrist):

- "'he will speak out against the Most High,'"

- he will "'wear down the saints of the Highest One'" (see also v. 21),

- "'he will intend to make alterations in times and in law'"; in other words, he will try to change the calendar and legal system (compare 2:21),

- he will dominate the world for "'a time, times, and half a time'" (three and a half years),

- in the end, God will destroy him forever.

Then the Lord will establish His glorious kingdom:

> "'Then the sovereignty, the dominion, and the greatness of all the kingdoms under the whole heaven will be given to the people of the saints of the Highest One; His kingdom will be an everlasting kingdom, and all the dominions will serve and obey Him.'" (7:27; see also v. 22)

With a triumphant finish, the dream returns Daniel to his own world, leaving him dazed by the amazing and terrible sights he has seen.

> "At this point the revelation ended. As for me, Daniel, my thoughts were greatly alarming me and my face grew pale, but I kept the matter to myself." (v. 28)

9. For more information on the EEC and its umbrella organization, the European Communities (EC), see Charles H. Dyer, "The EEC and European Unity," in World News and Bible Prophecy (Wheaton, Ill.: Tyndale House Publishers, n.d.), pp. 185–206.

The Vision Applied

As the dream drops us at the doorstep to our world, we hold in our hands four lessons—two from history and two from personal experience.

First, *since the first three kingdoms have arisen just as God predicted, we can be sure the fourth will follow suit.* The past reality of Babylon, Medo-Persia, and Greece ensure the future reality of the final, Romish kingdom. We can count all the events taking place as Daniel saw them—the confederacy of nations, the world dictator, the persecution of the saints, the judgment of God, and the wonders of the kingdom.

Second, *since the nations were established by God, they dwell under His sovereign control.* His prophetic collage may be confusing to us, but it's not to Him. He's sovereign over every detail.

Third, *the God who has mapped out the future is able to handle the present.* Your problems may be as difficult to sort out as Daniel's dream, but God is a specialist in revealing "the profound and hidden things" (2:22). He can help you make sense of your situation.

Fourth, *while life may appear to be a collage, it is, in reality, the unfolding of a perfect plan.* The angel pointed Daniel in the right direction, namely, the glory to come. The jumbled pieces in society and even in our lives will one day come together in a beautiful portrait that reflects and exalts the One who truly has dominion, Jesus Christ.

 *Living Insights*

Sometimes we get so close to God's prophetic collage that we lose sight of the big picture. For a moment, take a step back from the passage, like you might stand at a distance from a large mural at a museum. How does it strike you? What emotions does it touch?

_____

_____

What message is the Artist trying to communicate through the images on the canvas? You may want to review verses 9–10, 13–14, 17–18, 22, and 26–27.

_____

What comfort does this message give you?

_____

_____

Does this collage help you see God in a new way? How so?

_____

_____

_____

In what ways does this work of prophetic art inspire you to a closer walk with the Lord?

_____

_____

_____

_____

To help crystallize the encouragement and hope in Daniel's vision, take in the joy of Ronald Wallace's words:

> One of the main thrusts of the meaning of the passage is . . . clear. At the end the triumph will not be with the forces represented in the beast-kingdoms with all their inhumanity, but with that which is represented in the "son of man" figure. The coming kingdom will inevitably belong not to those who believe in oppression and cruelty, whose gospel is blind brute force, whose policy leads to the perversion of what is truly humane and good. The face of man may become obliterated for a season, for one or two generations or perhaps even three, but it will all reassert itself in the end. The son of man will come in the clouds of heaven![10]

10. Wallace, *The Message of Daniel*, p. 126.

Chapter 11

THE FINAL WORLD DICTATOR

Selected Scriptures

Daniel 7 provided our first introduction to the Antichrist—which is actually the first time he is mentioned in all of Scripture. There he is pictured symbolically as a boastful little horn with a shrewd intellect, having sprung from a beast so terrible it defied description.

Probably, some more literal images come to mind when you think of the Antichrist. Do you picture a shadowy, villainous figure—like something out of a 1930s horror movie? Or a Hitler-like madman raving into a microphone to a frenzied audience? Or maybe a devilish character with dark, sunken eyes and a satanic emblem on his chest?

As interesting as our speculations are, the more important question is, How does Scripture portray the Antichrist? Before we move on to Daniel 8, we need to dig a little deeper into the life of this man so that we can be discerning and not jump to conclusions about who will be the world's final and fiercest dictator.

General Information about the Antichrist

To begin, let's clear up a few misconceptions about his style and impact.

He Will Be Wanted, Not Rejected

First, people will *want* him to be their leader—which seems irrational to us. We can't imagine why anyone would willingly hand over their freedom to another person. Yet in desperate times, hungry, frightened people will eagerly follow anyone who offers them a solution and a hope. The citizens of Nazi Germany proved that.

Does the idea of a one-world dictator sound impossible to you? Look around. Crime rates are not just rising, they're out of control. Cities are overcrowded. Races are clashing. Economies are faltering. People are homeless and starving. We're ripe for the picking by any leader who can convince the nations that he has all the answers.

He Will Be Appealing, Not Repulsive

Second, he will attract people like honey draws bees. Because

Scripture uses names like "the beast," "the lawless one," and "the Antichrist," we assume he will be repulsive. But that's not so. Commentator James Montgomery Boice points out that the name *Antichrist* doesn't mean "opposite of Christ" but "instead of Christ." The implication is profound.

> Antichrist will be a substitute for Christ, as much like Christ as is possible for a tool of Satan. He will talk about justice and love, peace and prosperity. He will be brilliant and eloquent. In short, he will appear as an angel of light, as Satan himself often does, and will be hailed by millions as a superman who will save mankind.[1]

This leads us to a third fact.

He Will Be Super, Not Ordinary

The Antichrist will possess extraordinary abilities. He'll probably have the oratory skills and charm of John F. Kennedy, the inspirational power of Churchill, the vision of Marx, the dedication of Gandhi, the military prowess of Douglas MacArthur, the winsomeness of Will Rogers, the genius of Einstein, the esteem of Lincoln. *Time* magazine will name him Man of the Millennium. He will be the ultimate man . . . Satan will see to that.

He Will Be a Gentile, Not a Jew

Finally, it's helpful to remember that the Antichrist will be a Gentile. You may recall that all the beasts in Daniel 7 came out of the sea, which was a symbol for the Gentile nations (vv. 2–3).

Specific Scriptures Describing the Antichrist

Having gained a clearer overall perspective of this man, let's now delve into some specific portraits delineated in other Scripture passages.

The Little Horn in Daniel 7

Returning to Daniel 7, we discover that, according to verse 24, the little horn "will arise after [the ten kings]." No fanfare. No grand entrance. He will arise quietly, carefully, and within the natural course of events.

---

1. James Montgomery Boice, *The Last and Future World* (Grand Rapids, Mich.: Zondervan Publishing House, 1974), p. 70.

Once in power, his evil nature will become obvious:

> "'He will speak out against the Most High and wear
> down the saints of the Highest One.'" (v. 25a)

These believers are sometimes called the Tribulation saints, because they will come to Christ after the Rapture, during the Tribulation period.[2] The Antichrist will beat them down with a hailstorm of persecution. In Daniel 8, the prophet is given an even more emphatic description of what will come. (We'll learn more about these images from Daniel 8 in our next chapter.)

> "A king will arise
> Insolent and skilled in intrigue.
> And his power will be mighty, but not by his
> own power,
> And he will destroy to an extraordinary degree
> And prosper and perform his will;
> He will destroy mighty men and the holy people.
> And through his shrewdness
> He will cause deceit to succeed by his influence;
> And he will magnify himself in his heart,
> And he will destroy many while they are at ease."
> (vv. 23b–25a)

The world has never seen the sort of persecution the Antichrist will inflict on believers in the Tribulation.

In 2 Thessalonians, Paul aptly calls him "the son of destruction." Let's turn there next.

The Son of Destruction in 2 Thessalonians

> Now we request you, brethren, with regard to the coming of our Lord Jesus Christ, and our gathering together to Him, that you may not be quickly shaken from your composure or be disturbed either by a spirit or a message or a letter as if from us, to the effect that the day of the Lord has come. (2 Thess. 2:1–2)

---

2. Why do we believe that the church will be raptured before the Tribulation? (1) In 1 Thessalonians 4:13–18, Paul implies that the Rapture is the next event in God's prophetic plan. (2) The sudden and unexpected nature of Christ's return indicates that the Rapture must come first (Luke 12:40). And (3) Christ's promise to the church: "I also will keep you from the hour of testing, that hour which is about to come upon the whole world" (Rev. 3:10).

Suffering intensely, the Thessalonian believers were afraid that they had missed the Rapture and were living in the Tribulation period. Paul pulls in the reins on their runaway panic by saying,

> Let no one in any way deceive you, for it will not come unless the apostasy comes first. (v. 3a)

Apostasy indicates a general atmosphere that will surround the Antichrist's coming. It speaks of a world that will turn away from the things of God. And, more specifically, it signals a time when some who have professed Christ will depart from their Lord and His Word, spiraling down into error and sin.

> And the man of lawlessness is revealed, the son of destruction, who opposes and exalts himself above every so-called god or object of worship, so that he takes his seat in the temple of God, displaying himself as being God. (vv. 3b–4)

Move over God, here comes the Antichrist! Holding all the political strings in the world won't be enough for him. He'll grab the religious strings as well, the ones that lead straight to the people's hearts. A one-world religion is what he will be after, with himself as its god.

How will he convince the world he is divine? John tells us in Revelation 13.

The Beast in Revelation 13

In John's vision, he saw the Antichrist as a beast coming out of the sea, having

> ten horns and seven heads, and on his horns were ten diadems, and on his heads were blasphemous names. And the beast which I saw was like a leopard, and his feet were like those of a bear, and his mouth like the mouth of a lion. And the dragon gave him his power and his throne and great authority. (Rev. 13:1–2)

Many of the symbols from Daniel's vision reappear in John's. The Antichrist's empire will combine the greatness of the kingdoms of the past: the lion, bear, and leopard. The heads, crowns, and names illustrate his supreme authority on earth—authority derived from Satan himself, the dragon.

Satan's long-standing desire has been to set up his own kingdom on earth. After the Rapture, with the restraining influence of the church removed (2 Thess. 2:6–8), Satan will scheme a way to win the hearts of the people and steal the glory meant for God.

> And I saw one of his heads as if it had been slain, and his fatal wound was healed. And the whole earth was amazed and followed after the beast. (Rev. 13:3)

Perhaps as the result of an assassination attempt, the Beast will appear to die—but not really, for John says he saw the Beast "*as if it had been slain.*" Satan will counterfeit Christ's resurrection by healing the Beast's fatal wound, duping the world into thinking he has risen from the dead. In this way, Satan and the Antichrist will imitate the Father and the Son and steal the heart of humankind.

> And they worshiped the dragon [Satan], because he gave his authority to the beast; and they worshiped the beast, saying, "Who is like the beast, and who is able to wage war with him?" (v. 4)

Seated on the throne of Satan's kingdom, the pretender will speak blasphemies against God and attempt to crush God's people (vv. 5–7a). He will receive "authority over every tribe and people and tongue and nation," and "all who dwell on the earth will worship him" (vv. 7b, 8a).

John saw a third member of this unholy trinity—"another beast coming up out of the earth" (v. 11). Called the false prophet (19:20) and considered by some to be a Jew, this beast will perform "great signs, so that he even makes fire come down out of heaven" (13:13). He will order the people to build an idol of the Antichrist and will make it speak. Everyone who does not worship the image will be killed (vv. 14–15).

In addition, he will devise an economic system in which only the followers of the Antichrist will be allowed to buy or sell.

> And he causes all, the small and the great, and the rich and the poor, and the free men and the slaves, to be given a mark on their right hand, or on their forehead, and he provides that no one should be able to buy or to sell, except the one who has the mark, either the name of the beast or the number of his name. (vv. 16–17)

If you don't worship the Beast, you won't get a mark—perhaps a number or code—and you can't buy food. It's a devious way to persecute those who remain faithful to God.

God, however, has designed his own mark for the Antichrist:

> Here is wisdom. Let him who has understanding calculate the number of the beast, for the number is that of a man; and his number is six hundred and sixty-six. (v. 18)

For centuries, people have tried to decode this clue in order to unlock the identity of the Antichrist; but like a key in a jammed lock, it has refused to yield any results. God probably meant it for the Tribulation believers. When the time is right, He will open the lock and the believers will be able to use the numbers to identify the Beast and be warned. It will also serve as a reminder that, as powerful as he is, he is not above God. God has his number, and his number will soon be up.

The End of the Beast in Revelation 19

After a reign of terror lasting three and a half years, the impostor's judgment day will finally come when he meets the true Son of God face-to-face.

> And I saw the beast and the kings of the earth and their armies, assembled to make war against Him who sat upon the horse, and against His army. And the beast was seized, and with him the false prophet who performed the signs in his presence, by which he deceived those who had received the mark of the beast and those who worshiped his image; these two were thrown alive into the lake of fire which burns with brimstone. And the rest were killed with the sword which came from the mouth of Him who sat upon the horse, and all the birds were filled with their flesh. (Rev. 19:19–21)

With a crash of judgment, the Antichrist's dark storm will end. God's kingdom will take over Satan's kingdom, and a rainbow of hope will arch across the sky as Christ takes His seat on the throne as King of the earth (Isa. 9:2–7).

Concluding Suggestions regarding the Antichrist

Three words of advice emerge from our study of the Antichrist. First, *watch the news with a keen eye on the Middle East.* As the time approaches for the Antichrist to appear, Israel will be in the center of world affairs more and more.

Second, *interpret current events with a mind on prophetic truth.* Knowing that each event is part of a larger plan helps us remain calm in the midst of chaos. Political and economic earthquakes may shake us, but they won't tear us down.

Third, *anticipate Christ's coming with a heart on God's promise— the Rapture of the church.* We have no reason to fear the Antichrist or the wave of events that God has planned for the future, because we know how our story ends—in glory.

> For the Lord Himself will descend from heaven with a shout, with the voice of the archangel, and with the trumpet of God; and the dead in Christ shall rise first. Then we who are alive and remain shall be caught up together with them in the clouds to meet the Lord in the air, and thus we shall always be with the Lord. Therefore comfort one another with these words. (1 Thess. 4:16–18)

 Living Insights

Everything the human heart yearns for in a savior, the Antichrist will seem to provide. He will unite our splintered world, bring justice and order, even appear to conquer our final enemy— death. Like the legendary Pied Piper, he will play his tune of hope and happiness and lead humankind dancing all the way to destruction.

The apostle John warns us that, in the last days, there will be many antichrists who, like the final Antichrist, will lead people away from the truth. What is the surefire way we can spot one of these false teachers (see 1 John 2:18–22)?

MATH 24:

What popular religions or philosophies of today deny Christ as the Son of God?

mormans, Jahove, Hindu,

What is it about these religions and philosophies that attracts followers?

Have you ever felt the lure to abandon Christianity for one of these substitutes? How has it appealed to you?

Would not have to Go to the Cross

How can you keep yourself from getting tangled in the web of false doctrine (see v. 24)?

Do you need to be more firmly grounded in the truth of Scripture? If so, you might want to develop a game plan for digging in and really studying God's Word. One of the Gospels, perhaps John, would be a good place to start. And if you accompanied this with the book of Romans, you would soon have a good grasp on Jesus' identity and the tenets of our Christian faith.[3]

After that, work through Matthew's gospel—keep rooting yourself in who Jesus is and what His kingdom is about. Paul's letters to the Galatians and Ephesians will provide a nice complement.

God's Word, Old Testament and New, is a gift meant to be opened . . . savored . . . imbibed . . . incarnated. There's no better defense against deception than to be living the truth.

3. For an overview of the main themes in Romans, see the six-chapter study guide *Classic Truths for Triumphant Living*, coauthored by Bryce Klabunde, from the Bible-teaching ministry of Charles R. Swindoll (Anaheim, Calif.: Insight for Living, 1996).

Chapter 12

THE LIVING END
Daniel 8

With a clearer concept of the Antichrist in mind, let's get digging in Daniel again. In chapter 8, Daniel has another vision; the animals in this one aren't quite as disturbing as those in chapter 7, but the more detailed foreshadowing of the Antichrist is.

Introduction and Setting

Two years have passed since Daniel's last vision (chap. 7). It is now "the third year of the reign of Belshazzar" (8:1), and Daniel is probably in his early seventies. In this vision, Daniel sees himself "in the citadel of Susa, which is in the province of Elam," situated "beside the Ulai Canal" (v. 2).

Let's not miss the significance of this place. Located about two hundred miles east of Babylon, Susa belonged to the Babylonians' archenemies, the Persians. In another twelve years, they would join the Medes to overthrow Belshazzar and rule the empire (see Dan. 5). To underscore this change, God sets Daniel's vision in Susa—the upcoming center of world power.

No one in Daniel's day could have imagined the fall of Babylon and Susa's role in the unfolding drama of history.[1] Only Daniel would preview these incredible events.

Revelation and Significance

Daniel's vision has two major elements in it: first, the ram and the goat; and second, the little horn.

The Ram and the Goat

As the vision develops, Daniel sees a ram with two horns standing in front of the canal. The horns are unique, for one is "longer than the other, with the longer one coming up last" (8:3). Daniel watches it battle other animals:

> I saw the ram butting westward, northward, and

1. On this same site, the courageous queen Esther would intercede for the lives of her people (see Esther 1:2); and the rebuilder of Jerusalem's walls, Nehemiah, would serve as cupbearer to king Artaxerxes (see Neh. 1:1).

southward, and no other beasts could stand before him, nor was there anyone to rescue from his power; but he did as he pleased and magnified himself. (v. 4)

Before Daniel can take his eyes off the ram, a male goat with "a conspicuous horn between his eyes" suddenly appears in the west, racing "over the surface of the whole earth without touching the ground" (v. 5). "In his mighty wrath," he charges the ram (v. 6).

And I saw him come beside the ram, and he was enraged at him; and he struck the ram and shattered his two horns, and the ram had no strength to withstand him. So he hurled him to the ground and trampled on him, and there was none to rescue the ram from his power. Then the male goat magnified himself exceedingly. (vv. 7–8a)

The victory celebration doesn't last long, however.

As soon as he was mighty, the large horn was broken; and in its place there came up four conspicuous horns toward the four winds of heaven. (v. 8b)

The Little Horn

From one of these four "conspicuous" horns a small horn emerges and grows "exceedingly great toward the south, toward the east, and toward the Beautiful Land"—that is, Palestine (v. 9). As this little horn's power increases, it turns vicious, and its pride ascends to tremendous heights.

And it grew up to the host of heaven and caused some of the host and some of the stars to fall to the earth, and it trampled them down. It even magnified itself to be equal with the Commander of the host; and it removed the regular sacrifice from Him, and the place of His sanctuary was thrown down. (vv. 10–11)

It boasts in God's face, desecrates the temple, mistreats God's people ("the host") . . . and seems to get away with it!

And on account of transgression the host will be given over to the horn along with the regular sacrifice; and it will fling truth to the ground and perform its will and prosper. (v. 12)

96

Then Daniel hears one angel ask another:

> "How long will the vision about the regular sacrifice apply, while the transgression causes horror, so as to allow both the holy place and the host to be trampled?" (v. 13)

The answer resounds from the other angel, "For 2,300 evenings and mornings; then the holy place will be properly restored" (v. 14). This number probably refers to the regular sacrifices, which were offered every evening and morning. So for 2,300 sacrifices, or 1,150 days (a little over three years), the little horn will shut down temple worship and terrorize the Jewish nation.

The Interpretation

As Daniel struggles to understand the images, a figure appears before him, "one who looked like a man" (v. 15). Then a voice identifies the figure: "Gabriel, give this man an understanding of the vision" (v. 16). God has dispatched His special messenger from heaven to Daniel.

> So he came near to where I was standing, and when he came I was frightened and fell on my face; but he said to me, "Son of man, understand that the vision pertains to the time of the end." Now while he was talking with me, I sank into a deep sleep with my face to the ground; but he touched me and made me stand upright. And he said, "Behold, I am going to let you know what will occur at the final period of the indignation, for it pertains to the appointed time of the end." (vv. 17–19)

Gabriel alerts both Daniel and us that, while the vision is partially about historical kings and kingdoms, it also looks beyond to the ultimate end of time. This is called a "double fulfillment," where the near fulfillment of the prophecy foreshadows the far. Both aspects will become apparent as Gabriel interprets the vision.

The Meaning of the Ram

The angel begins by explaining what the ram symbolizes.

> "The ram which you saw with the two horns represents

the kings of Media and Persia."[2] (v. 20)

Reminiscent of the bear with one side raised up (7:5), the ram that Daniel saw had one horn more prominent than the other, the longer emerging after the shorter. In a similar way, Persia arose after Media but eventually took the superior role. With a vast army of more than two million soldiers, the Persian kings mercilessly rammed their enemies, expanding the empire west to Macedonia, north past the Caspian Sea, and south through Egypt.[3]

For about two hundred years, the ram ruled the world and boasted of its seeming invincibility—until a charging force from the west knocked it from its pinnacle of power.

The Meaning of the Goat

The angel continues,

> "And the shaggy goat represents the kingdom of Greece, and the large horn that is between his eyes is the first king." (8:21)

The single large horn between the goat's eyes represents Alexander the Great, the young military genius who stormed through the Persian empire with his small but highly disciplined army. Told by his mother that his father, Philip of Macedon, descended from Hercules, Alexander grew up determined to accomplish his own Herculean task. With unprecedented speed, he conquered Asia Minor, Syria, Egypt, and Mesopotamia. Within three years, Alexander had crushed all of Persia, converted the culture to Hellenism, and was pushing on to India.[4]

The one foe he could not conquer, however, was his addiction to alcohol. In 323 B.C., at age 33, Alexander died from a fever brought on by malaria and complications from alcoholism. At the height of his power, the mighty horn was broken.

---

2. Historians tell us that the Medo-Persian armies marched under a flag with a ram on it. See M.R. DeHaan, *Daniel—the Prophet* (Grand Rapids, Mich.: Zondervan Publishing House, 1972), p. 220.

3. J. Dwight Pentecost, "Daniel," in *The Bible Knowledge Commentary*, Old Testament edition, ed. John F. Walvoord and Roy B. Zuck (Wheaton, Ill.: Scripture Press, Victor Books, 1985), p. 1356, see maps on p. 1352.

4. Gleason L. Archer, Jr., "Daniel," in *The Expositor's Bible Commentary*, gen. ed. Frank E. Gaebelein (Grand Rapids, Mich.: Zondervan Publishing House, Regency Reference Library, 1985), vol. 7, p. 97.

The Meaning of the Four Horns

With two future kingdoms unveiled, Gabriel goes on to tell Daniel what will happen next.

> "And the broken horn and the four horns that arose
> in its place represent four kingdoms which will arise
> from his nation, although not with his power." (v. 22)

After years of infighting, Alexander's four generals divided the kingdom: Cassander took Macedonia and Greece; Lysimachus, Thrace and parts of Asia Minor; Ptolemy, Egypt and parts of Asia Minor; and Seleucus, Syria, Israel, and Mesopotamia. For years, the generals and their successors would battle each other for total control, but none of them would rise to the same level of power as Alexander.

The Meaning of the Little Horn—Past

Now we've reached the little horn of verses 9–12 and the double fulfillment mentioned earlier. For in the following description of a coming leader, Antiochus IV Epiphanes, we also see the ultimate Antichrist.

> "And in the latter period of their rule,
> When the transgressors have run their course,
> A king will arise
> Insolent and skilled in intrigue.
> And his power will be mighty, but not by his
> own power,
> And he will destroy to an extraordinary degree
> And prosper and perform his will;
> He will destroy mighty men and the holy people.
> And through his shrewdness
> He will cause deceit to succeed by his influence;
> And he will magnify himself in his heart,
> And he will destroy many while they are at ease.
> He will even oppose the Prince of princes,
> But he will be broken without human agency.
> And the vision of the evenings and mornings
> Which has been told is true;
> But keep the vision secret,
> For it pertains to many days in the future."
> (vv. 23–26)

Out of the Seleucid dynasty sprouted the little horn, Antiochus IV Epiphanes, who ruled from 175 to 163 B.C. The name *Epiphanes* means "the Illustrious One," which gives you an idea of the size of this man's ego. The Jews called him Antiochus *Epimanes*, which means "the Madman."[5] He was a madman—an ancient Hitler who rolled like a Panzer tank across Israel and through Egypt. On one occasion, notes J. Dwight Pentecost,

> Antiochus sent his general Apollonius with 22,000 soldiers into Jerusalem on what was purported to be a peace mission. But they attacked Jerusalem on the Sabbath, killed many people, took many women and children as slaves, and plundered and burned the city.[6]

Determined to Hellenize (make Greek) his world, he tightened his iron grip on the Jews, attempting to wipe out the Hebrew religion and convert their temple into a place of pagan worship. Commentator W. A. Criswell chronicles his abominable deeds.

> He took a sow and offered it on the great, brazen altar spreading the juice of it all over the temple and the sacred vessels. In that way he defiled everything in the eyes of a Mosaic Jew. He forbade the Jewish festivals and feasts. Instead of the Feast of Tabernacles, Passover, or Pentecost, he celebrated in the temple the Bacchanalia, worshiping Bacchus, the god of pleasure and wine. He forced the Jews to observe the Saturnalia, worshiping Saturn, using harlots in the temple itself for those feast days. He forbade the observance of the Sabbath. He not only forbade the reading of the Scriptures but he burned the sacred books. He forbade the institution of circumcision. There were two mothers who circumcised their babies in defiance of his law. He took those two babies, slew them, hung each one around its mother's neck, marched the women through the streets of Jerusalem up to the highest wall and flung them headlong to death.[7]

---

5. Pentecost, "Daniel," p. 1358.

6. Pentecost, "Daniel," p. 1370.

7. W. A. Criswell, *Expository Sermons on the Book of Daniel*, 4 vols. in one (Grand Rapids, Mich.: Zondervan Publishing House, 1976), vol. 4, p. 79.

It was a horrible era in Jewish history. However, Antiochus' desecration would end just as the angel predicted. Three years after Antiochus profaned the temple in late 167,

> [Judas Maccabaeus] "refurbished and rededicated the temple, restoring the daily sacrifices in Chislev 25 (14 December 164 B.C.). . . . This marked the commencement of the Jewish Feast of Dedication (or Lights) (Heb., *Hanukkah*)."[8]

Soon after, Antiochus "the Madman" died insane.

The Meaning of the Little Horn—Future

Even though much of Daniel 8:23–26 matches Antiochus IV Epiphanes' reign of terror, some of the prophecy quite obviously goes beyond him—to someone even more powerful and evil, the Antichrist. Let's take a look at these particular descriptions.

In verse 24, we're told, "His power will be mighty, but not by his own power." The Antichrist's power will come from the force of great darkness, Satan himself.

Also, at the end of verse 25, the Antichrist is shown to "even oppose the Prince of princes." He will directly challenge Jesus, the destroyer's archenemy. However, "he will be broken without human agency"; meaning he will suffer terrible judgment from the very hand of God.

What Antiochus was to the Jews, the Antichrist will be to believers in the Tribulation and more. Cunning . . . malicious . . . deadly. Like a snake in the grass, he will rise up and strike God's people over and over with vicious tenacity. What human can stand against him?

The chart on page 102 summarizes Daniel 8 and illustrates how the prophecies lead up to the Antichrist.

The Reaction

The grim images of future affliction are enough to make Daniel "exhausted and sick for days" (v. 27a). He finally resumes his duties, but he can't shake the nightmare. He concludes his account with

---

8. H. W. Hoehner, "Antiochus I/Antiochus VII," in *The Zondervan Pictorial Encyclopedia of the Bible*, gen. ed. Merrill C. Tenney (Grand Rapids, Mich.: Zondervan Publishing House, Regency Reference Library, 1976), vol. 1, p. 193.

History and Prophecy in Daniel 8

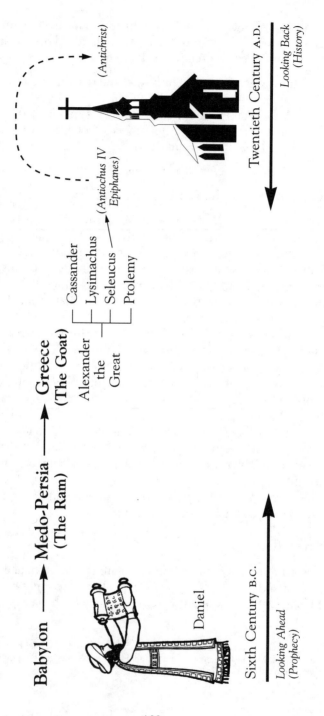

Babylon → Medo-Persia → Greece
(The Ram)   (The Goat)

Cassander
Lysimachus
Seleucus — (Antiochus IV
Ptolemy   Epiphanes)

Alexander
the
Great

(Antichrist)

Daniel

Sixth Century B.C.

*Looking Ahead
(Prophecy)*

Twentieth Century A.D.

*Looking Back
(History)*

a tone of confusion and dismay:

> Then I got up again and carried on the king's business; but I was astounded at the vision, and there was none to explain it. (v. 27b)

Viewing the vision from our historical vantage point, our reactions might vary from his. Rather than being dismayed, *we might gain confidence in God's Word.* The precise fulfillment of the prophecies can reassure us that God's Word is true and dependable. Since God's promises have been fulfilled in the past, we can trust His power to take care of our present.

However, like Daniel, *we might become fearful.* If Antiochus is only a shadow of the Antichrist, what horrors await us in the future? Thinking of them is enough to make us exhausted and sick too. Yet in Revelation 3:10, Christ offers a calming promise:

> "'Because you have kept the word of My perseverance, I also will keep you from the hour of testing, that hour which is about to come upon the whole world, to test those who dwell upon the earth.'"

Our hope is in Jesus, who will deliver us from the *Epimanes* to come, whomever he may be.

Finally, this vision of the future should encourage us to *share with others the promise of salvation.* The bright beam of hope that shines through the vision is that the Antichrist, along with every force that flings itself against God, "will be broken" (Dan. 8:25). Do you know people who are fighting the Lord? Their lives don't have to end up shattered on the judgment stone of God. Having died for them on the cross, Christ offers His life for theirs. It's a grace exchange that promises salvation from the wrath to come. Won't you shine His light of hope their way today?

 Living Insights

Funny thing about hurricanes. They can linger offshore for days, spinning, shifting, stalling. You know they're out there, but you're never quite sure when they'll strike. The best strategy is to keep informed, stay prepared, and warn your neighbors.

We can use a similar strategy as we face the end-times hurricane that looms off the coast of world events. You're already following the first step by studying the book of Daniel. You can also keep informed by reading good books on the subject. We've recommended a few in the Books for Probing Further section at the end of this study guide.

How can we stay prepared? By fortifying our relationship with Christ. When He comes to rescue us at the Rapture, we want to be ready. Are there some loose planks in your spiritual life that you need to nail down? What can you do to be ready for the Savior?

_____

_____

_____

_____

_____

Finally, we can warn our neighbors. As dark as the prophetical skies are these days, many people around us are living as if the sun is shining and life will keep on going without interruption. Whom do you need to warn about the coming "hurricane"?

_____

_____

_____

None of us wants to be here when the Antichrist blows onto the scene. Let's try to take as many people as we can to heaven with us at the Rapture. That's the safest place to be.

Chapter 13

TRUE CONFESSIONS
Daniel 9:1–19

"G ive me a place on which to stand, and I will move the earth," said Archimedes about the power of the lever.[1] Couldn't we say something similar about prayer—"Give us a place on which to kneel, and we can move the world"?

Do you *really* believe that? Given today's state of moral decay, it would seem easier to change the earth's rotation than a nation's heart, wouldn't it?

Yet Daniel believed in the power of prayer . . . because he believed in the power of God. As only one person, he pleaded with God on behalf of all his people, and he was heard. Whether we pray for the needs of an individual or a whole country, we can learn from Daniel's example of intercessory prayer.

Setting for Daniel's Prayer

As in all of his previous chapters, Daniel begins by placing events in their historical context:

> In the first year of Darius the son of Ahasuerus,
> of Median descent, who was made king over the
> kingdom of the Chaldeans. (Dan. 9:1)

More than a decade has passed since Daniel's last prophetic vision (chap. 8). Belshazzar has perished, just as the handwriting on the wall predicted, and Babylon's faded glory has become Medo-Persia's victorious fanfare.

With the old government in shambles, the new king has a lot of rebuilding to do. In the middle of the construction project, covered with the dust of change, stands Daniel reading a set of blueprints. Plans for the new empire? No, he's studying God's design for Israel.

In the first year of his reign I, Daniel, observed in

---

1. Archimedes, *The Little, Brown Book of Anecdotes,* ed. Clifton Fadiman (Boston, Mass.: Little, Brown and Co., 1985), p. 19. Archimedes was an ancient Greek mathematician, physicist, and inventor.

the books the number of the years which was revealed as the word of the Lord to Jeremiah the prophet for the completion of the desolations of Jerusalem, namely, seventy years. (9:2)

Jeremiah 25 was probably the passage he was reading:

"Therefore thus says the Lord of hosts, 'Because you have not obeyed My words, behold, I will send and take all the families of the north,' declares the Lord, 'and I will send to Nebuchadnezzar king of Babylon, My servant, and will bring them against this land, and against its inhabitants, and against all these nations round about; and I will utterly destroy them, and make them a horror, and a hissing, and an everlasting desolation. Moreover, I will take from them the voice of joy and the voice of gladness, the voice of the bridegroom and the voice of the bride, the sound of the millstones and the light of the lamp. And this whole land shall be a desolation and a horror, and these nations shall serve the king of Babylon seventy years.'"[2] (vv. 8–11; see also 29:1–20)

How many years had it been since Daniel had seen his homeland? He'd been brought to Babylon as a youth, and now he was an old man. About sixty-six years had gone by—Jeremiah's seventy years were almost up. But, Daniel wondered, were his people ready to return to Israel, God's covenant land?

In the midst of his new administrative duties (see Dan. 6:1–3), Daniel stopped to pray for his nation, which needed it now more than ever.

Ingredients in Daniel's Prayer

So I gave my attention to the Lord God to seek Him by prayer and supplications, with fasting, sackcloth, and ashes. (9:3)

2. Why did Jeremiah predict seventy years? God had instructed His people not only to observe a weekly Sabbath for themselves but also to give the land a Sabbath rest every seven years (Lev. 25:2–7). If they disobeyed, the Lord would remove them from the land so it could have its rest (Lev. 26:34–35). Apparently, Israel deprived the land of seventy Sabbaths; thus they were driven into captivity for seventy years, and the land finally had its rest (2 Chron. 36:20–21).

As Daniel prays, five attitudes blend together to make the fragrance of his prayer pleasing to the Lord.

1. *Concentration.* In giving his attention to and seeking the Lord, Daniel *concentrates* on Him. How vital this is, yet how difficult! Poet and preacher John Donne wrote:

> I throw myself down in my chamber, and I call in and invite God and his angels thither, and when they are there, I neglect God and his angels, for the noise of a fly, for the rattling of a coach, for the whining of a door.[3]

Reading Scripture, as Daniel did before he prayed, can help focus our thoughts and guard against distractions.

2. *Supplication.* Daniel also sought the Lord "by prayer and supplications," which pictures a servant kneeling and pleading his or her case before a king. This kind of prayer is passionate and vulnerable; it involves our whole being—heart, mind, and body.

3. *Self-Denial.* By seeking the Lord "with fasting," Daniel denied himself an ordinary, daily function to give himself to God in prayer. Fasting is essentially a method of prioritizing. It's a way of saying to God that He is more important than everything else, even things that give us life and pleasure.

4. *Humility.* While fasting, Daniel put on sackcloth and ashes, a sign of deep sorrow and humility. He was not like the self-righteous Pharisee, who thanked God for his being better than others (Luke 18:9–12). Rather, Daniel approached the Lord as the tax-gatherer did, acutely aware of his and his people's sinfulness and their need for their holy God's mercy (vv. 13–14; see also Dan. 9:18b).

5. *Honesty.* Throughout Daniel's prayer, he never once glosses over or tries to find excuses for his sins and those of his fellow Jews. In fact, he takes on his nation's sins as if they were his own. As we consider the content of his prayer, notice how he consistently includes himself with the pronoun *we.*

Content of Daniel's Prayer

Daniel's prayer pours out of his soul like a passionate symphony; its themes of praise and confession rise and fall as it climaxes toward

---

3. John Donne, as quoted in *Bartlett's Familiar Quotations*, 15th ed., rev. and enl., ed. Emily Morison Beck (Boston, Mass.: Little, Brown and Co., 1980), p. 255.

a finale of petition to the Lord. Take a few minutes to read verses 4–19 to feel the movement and emotion of his prayer. Then we'll see what the inspiring tones have to tell us.

Praise

Daniel never allows his heart's desires to obscure the One he bows before.

> And I prayed to the Lord my God and confessed and said, "Alas, O Lord, the great and awesome God, who keeps His covenant and lovingkindness for those who love Him and keep His commandments." (v. 4)

In verse 7, he declares, "Righteousness belongs to Thee, O Lord." He echoes this in verse 14b: "For the Lord our God is righteous in respect to all His deeds which He has done." And in verse 9, he says, "To the Lord our God belong compassion and forgiveness."

These qualities give Daniel ground to stand on before the Lord, for he knows that, just as God is right to discipline His rebellious people, He is also eager to restore them when they come to Him in a spirit of repentance (see Jer. 29:10–14).

Confession

In contrast to the Lord's faithfulness and righteousness is His people's rebellion. Acting as a true intercessor, Daniel bears the sins of the nation before the Lord. His words, defined within brackets in the text, express the extent of Israel's failure.[4]

> "We have sinned [*missed the mark*], committed iniquity [*distorted God's Law*], acted wickedly [*done known wrong*], and rebelled [*defied authority*], even turning aside from Thy commandments and ordinances. Moreover, we have not listened to [*nor obeyed*] Thy servants the prophets, who spoke in Thy name to our kings, our princes, our fathers, and all the people of the land." (Dan. 9:5–6)

The brilliance of God's holiness exposes Israel's nakedness.

> "Righteousness belongs to Thee, O Lord, but to us

---

4. These definitions are based on Leon Wood's in *A Commentary on Daniel* (Grand Rapids, Mich.: Zondervan Publishing House, 1973), p. 236.

open shame, as it is this day—to the men of Judah, the inhabitants of Jerusalem, and all Israel, those who are nearby and those who are far away in all the countries to which Thou hast driven them, because of their unfaithful deeds which they have committed against Thee. Open shame belongs to us, O Lord, to our kings, our princes, and our fathers, because we have sinned against Thee." (vv. 7–8)

In spite of God's compassion and forgiveness, Daniel laments that

"we have rebelled against Him; nor have we obeyed the voice of the Lord our God, to walk in His teachings which He set before us through His servants the prophets. Indeed all Israel has transgressed Thy law and turned aside, not obeying Thy voice; so the curse has been poured out on us, along with the oath which is written in the law of Moses the servant of God, for we have sinned against Him." (vv. 9b–11)

Disregard for God's law is the root from which all of Israel's troubles have sprouted. According to the Mosaic covenant, God promised to bless them if they kept His law (see Deut. 28:1–14) and warned that He would curse them if they didn't (see vv. 15–68, especially vv. 36–37, 41, 49–52, 64–67). Moses told them,

"I call heaven and earth to witness against you today, that I have set before you life and death, the blessing and the curse. So choose life in order that you may live, you and your descendants, by loving the Lord your God, by obeying His voice, and by holding fast to Him." (30:19–20a)

Tragically, they chose death. Daniel confesses:

"Thus He has confirmed His words which He had spoken against us and against our rulers who ruled us, to bring on us great calamity; for under the whole heaven there has not been done anything like what was done to Jerusalem. As it is written in the law of Moses, all this calamity has come on us; yet we have not sought the favor of the Lord our God by turning from our iniquity and giving attention to Thy truth. Therefore, the Lord has kept the calamity in store and brought it on us; for the Lord our God is righteous with respect to all His deeds which He has done, but we have not obeyed His voice." (Dan. 9:12–14)

Thankfully, God is a God of redemption. Once before, He saved Israel from a foreign land, and Daniel concludes his confession with that picture of God rescuing His nation.

"And now, O Lord our God, who hast brought Thy people out of the land of Egypt with a mighty hand and hast made a name for Thyself, as it is this day— we have sinned, we have been wicked." (v. 15)

Petition

Having poured out his sorrow, Daniel presents two main petitions to God, one negative—to remove His wrath—and one positive—to grant His forgiveness.

"O Lord, in accordance with all Thy righteous acts, let now Thine anger and Thy wrath turn away from Thy city Jerusalem, Thy holy mountain; for because of our sins and the iniquities of our fathers, Jerusalem and Thy people have become a reproach to all those around us. So now, our God, listen to the prayer of Thy servant and to his supplications, and for Thy sake, O Lord, let Thy face shine on Thy desolate sanctuary. O my God, incline Thine ear and hear! Open Thine eyes and see our desolations and the city which is called by Thy name." (vv. 16–18a)

With priestly care, Daniel beseeches God to let His "face shine on" His temple (compare Num. 6:22–27). Why? Because the Jews have suffered enough and deserve God's blessing now? Not in Daniel's truthful mind.

"For we are not presenting our supplications before Thee on account of any merits of our own, but on account of Thy great compassion." (Dan. 9:18b)

Then, almost desperately, Daniel begs God to help:

"O Lord, hear! O Lord, forgive! O Lord, listen and take action! For Thine own sake, O my God, do not delay, because Thy city and Thy people are called by Thy name." (v. 19)

Daniel cries out not for his or his people's sake but for the Lord's sake. In his prayer and in his life, Daniel's primary passion is the glory of God.

Application of Daniel's Prayer

Israel's hope did not rest in what they had to offer God—rebellion, sin, and failure—but in God Himself. Where have we placed our hope as a nation? The economy, the courts, the police, the leaders . . . everywhere, it seems, but the Lord. Our money proclaims, "In God we trust." But do we, really?

The most powerful tool we can use to move our country toward repentance and godliness is the spiritual lever of prayer. In the Living Insights section, we'll use Daniel's prayer as a model for how to intercede for our community and nation. Can one person's prayers make a difference? Daniel's did, and yours can too.

 Living Insights

"This country's going down the tubes," we hear almost daily. We can do a lot more about it than moan and groan, though. If we really care about our country and its future, we can pray.

Let's begin by following Daniel's example.

Take a moment to review Daniel's five attitudes of prayer: concentration, supplication, self-denial, humility, and honesty. As you open yourself to God, remember to stay focused and guard yourself from distraction. Let God help you by listening to His Word (consider passages like Jer. 29:7; Matt. 5:1–16; 1 Tim. 2:1–4).

Also, remember who you are praying to—the Most High God, the King of Kings. His name is worth making sacrifices for, like skipping a meal or getting up early. And be humble about your motives; being honest about your sins will help with that.

Is your heart ready (not perfect—just prepared)? Then please, take some time to pray for your country.

Praise

• Give glory to God for His attributes (Dan. 9:4, 7, 9).

- Acknowledge the ways He has demonstrated His righteousness and compassion to your nation.

Confession

- Read Daniel's confessions in verses 5–15, inserting the name of your country and your government leaders.

- Lay before the Lord some specific sins of the community and nation you have personally witnessed.

Petition

- Build on Daniel's petitions as you read verses 16–19, elaborating on them in your own words.

- Offer some special requests to the Lord. Pray for presidents and prime ministers, parliaments and congresses. Pray for lawmakers and law enforcers, lawyers and judges. Pray for your local leaders. Pray for your school board, your children's schools, their teachers. Space is provided if you want to make a list.

_____

_____

_____

_____

_____

_____

 Digging Deeper

The Scriptures include at least five distinct categories of prayer. All five are ours to practice as children of God. To keep our times with the Lord fresh and free from routine, we should use all of these approaches on a regular basis with our heavenly Father.

There is no significance in the order with which the categories are listed below.

Category	Scripture	Explanation
Worship or Praise	1 Chron. 29:11–13 Ps. 146:1–2 Rom. 11:33–36 Rev. 4:10–11 Rev. 5:12–14	Expressing worth, adoration, and honor to God.
Confession	Pss. 32:5; 38:18 Pss. 51:1–3; 66:18 Prov. 28:13 1 John 1:9	Declaring openly and honestly our dis-obedience. Claiming God's forgiveness through the merits of Christ.
Thanksgiving	Ps. 138 Rom. 1:8 Eph. 5:20 1 Thess. 5:18	Acknowledging our gratitude to God for His blessings and pro-visions as well as His tests and discipline.
Intercession	1 Sam. 12:23 Eph. 1:18 1 Tim. 2:1–2 James 5:14–16	Supporting others in prayer . . . remem-bering their special needs.
Petition	Phil. 4:6–7 1 Thess. 5:17 Heb. 4:14–16 James 1:5	Expressing our own needs and requests to God.

One of the most convicting truths in all of Scripture is found in James 4:2b: "You do not have because you do not ask."

Have you asked?

———◆———

Notes on Prayer

_____

_____

_____

_____

_____

Chapter 14

THE BACKBONE OF
BIBLICAL PROPHECY

Daniel 9:20–27

"O Lord, hear! O Lord, forgive!" Daniel cries out to God, pleading for the salvation of his people (Dan. 9:19). As he fervently
prays, tears mingle with drops of sweat. Trembling concentration is
punctuated with loud wailing. Wringing himself out before the
Lord, Daniel is left limp and exhausted (see v. 21).

On the battleground of prayer, heroes are marked by their perseverance. As Daniel prays, the minutes melt into hours . . . the
day slips into the chilled shadows of twilight.

Does God hear His servant's pleas? Is there hope for Israel?

The Angelic Interruption

With the temple in ruins, Daniel has been offering *himself* on
the altar of prayer when a message arrives from heaven—delivered
by angelic courier.

> Now while I was speaking and praying, and con-
> fessing my sin and the sin of my people Israel, and
> presenting my supplication before the Lord my God
> in behalf of the holy mountain of my God, while I
> was still speaking in prayer, then the man Gabriel,
> whom I had seen in the vision previously, came to
> me in my extreme weariness about the time of the
> evening offering.[1] And he gave me instruction and
> talked with me, and said, "O Daniel, I have now
> come forth to give you insight with understanding."
> (Dan. 9:20–22)

Gabriel offers Daniel truth, or "insight," and the ability to understand that truth—but not before he assures him of his honored
position before the Lord.

---

1. This was probably one of Daniel's regular prayer times that got him thrown into the lions'
den in chapter 6. Could it be that the lions' den episode was Satan's attempt to stop Daniel
before he could intercede for Israel and receive the prophecy Gabriel was sent to deliver?

"At the beginning of your supplications the command was issued, and I have come to tell you, for you are highly esteemed; so give heed to the message and gain understanding of the vision." (v. 23)

God values the broken vessel. At Daniel's first word of repentance, God knew that *this* was the man He wanted to receive His message.

Considered the backbone of biblical prophecy, Gabriel's words to Daniel tie together the messianic and end-times prophecies that course through the body of Scripture. Daniel has been praying for the restoration of his people to their land of promise, but God has a bigger picture in mind—the promise of the coming Messiah and the ultimate restoration of the Jews.

The Seventy Weeks

Although Daniel doesn't realize it, he's standing at a critical juncture in Jewish history. As Israel's seventy-year captivity comes to an end, God is marking out for the Jews another block of time, which, interestingly, is also based on the number seventy.

One Block of Time

In verse 24, Gabriel spreads out the timeline before Daniel.

"Seventy weeks have been decreed for your people
and your holy city."

The Hebrew word translated *weeks* is a generic term meaning "sevens" or "units of seven." We normally associate a unit of seven with a week of seven days. But is the angel talking about days here?

A good rule of thumb in finding the meaning of a word is to look at the context. For instance, when we go to a doughnut shop and say, "I'll take a dozen," the clerk knows from the context that we're talking about a dozen doughnuts. Since Daniel's prayer concerns Israel's seventy-year captivity (v. 2), it makes sense that Gabriel's "weeks" are referring to years: seventy periods of seven-year units. God's next program for the Jews will be consummated in seventy years times seven—that is, 490 years.

Six Objectives

The rest of verse 24 tells us that, during this block of time, God will accomplish six objectives on behalf of His people. He will:

- "finish the transgression"

- "make an end of sin"

- "make atonement for iniquity"

- "bring in everlasting righteousness"

- "seal up vision and prophecy"

- "anoint the most holy place"

In His grace, God answers Daniel's prayer to forgive the Jews and return them to their homeland. But He does so much more! With the first three objectives, He offers permanent pardon for sins (compare Jer. 33:4–9); in the last three, a lasting home in His kingdom (compare vv. 14–18). The first three have already been fulfilled in Christ's coming, dying, and rising; the last three are waiting to be fulfilled at His return.

Three Divisions

The angel then slices the block of time into three sections: seven weeks (49 years), sixty-two weeks (434 years), and one week (7 years). Let's consider each in turn.

> "So you are to know and discern that from the issuing of a decree to restore and rebuild Jerusalem until Messiah the Prince there will be seven weeks and sixty-two weeks; it will be built again, with plaza and moat, even in times of distress." (Dan. 9:25)

How do we know which date to begin counting from? After all, several royal decrees were issued to the Jews over the years (see 2 Chron. 36:22–23; Ezra 1:1–4; 6:1–12; 7:11–26). Only one, however, was "to restore and rebuild Jerusalem" (Dan. 9:25a)— Artaxerxes' decree to Nehemiah (Neh. 2:1–8). Nehemiah gives us the date as "the month Nisan, in the twentieth year of King Artaxerxes" (v. 1), or March/April 444 B.C.[2] As Artaxerxes hands over the letters clearing Nehemiah's way to rebuild the holy city, the prophecy clock starts ticking.

The first division. The first time period spans "seven weeks" or

---

2. See Harold W. Hoehner, *Chronological Aspects of the Life of Christ* (Grand Rapids, Mich.: Zondervan Publishing House, Academie Books, 1977), p. 128. Other scholars believe the date is March/April 445 B.C.

forty-nine years, during which time Jerusalem will be completely rebuilt. The opposition that Nehemiah encountered would certainly qualify as "times of distress" (see 4:1–23; 6:1–9), but it took Nehemiah only fifty-two days to finish building the wall around Jerusalem (Neh. 6:15). The forty-nine-year period must refer to the time it took to reconstruct the entire city, "with plaza and moat."

The second division. When Jerusalem is rebuilt, Daniel's next time period will begin—the "sixty-two weeks." This span will culminate in the appearance of "Messiah the Prince" (Dan. 9:25). If we add the "seven weeks and sixty-two weeks" after Artaxerxes' decree, we get sixty-nine "weeks," or 483 years. By using the Jewish calendar, which is based on a 360-day lunar year, we discover that a 483-year period equals 173,880 days. According to New Testament scholar Harold Hoehner, by counting forward 173,880 days from the first of Nisan (March 5) 444 B.C. when Nehemiah received the decree, we arrive at Nisan 10 (March 30), A.D. 33—the very day Jesus entered Jerusalem as Messiah the Prince (see Luke 19:29–40).[3]

Amazing! Five centuries before the event, God drew an X on the exact date Jesus would appear as the long-awaited Son of David. On that momentous day, the people spread their garments on the road and shouted, "Blessed is the King who comes in the name of the Lord" (v. 38). An epic prophetic drama was being enacted on the stage of history, and nothing could stand in its way. When the Pharisees tried to stop the chorus, Jesus replied, "I tell you, if these become silent, the stones will cry out!" (v. 40).

In the bright spotlight of Daniel's prophecy, Jesus could hardly be missed. This was Jerusalem's golden day, the 173,880th day of Daniel's prophecy, and Jesus was prepared to fulfill all six objectives mentioned in Daniel 9:24. Incredibly, though, His own people refused Him. Approaching Jerusalem, the City of Peace, Jesus wept, "If you had known in this day, even you, the things which make for peace!" (v. 42a).

After centuries of sin and strife, the city could've finally realized the full meaning of its name. But because the people rejected their

---

3. Hoehner, *Chronological Aspects*, p. 138. The scholars who hold to a March 445 B.C. date for Artaxerxes' decree add 173,880 days and arrive at April 6, A.D. 32, which they conclude is the date of Jesus' triumphal entry. See Alva J. McClain, *Daniel's Prophecy of the 70 Weeks* (Grand Rapids, Mich.: Zondervan Publishing House, 1969), pp. 25–26. Those who hold to an A.D. 30 Crucifixion usually choose Artaxerxes' decree to Ezra in 458 B.C. as the beginning point and Jesus' baptism as the ending point, which they place in A.D. 26. See Leon Wood, *A Commentary on Daniel* (Grand Rapids, Mich.: Zondervan Publishing House, 1973), p. 253.

Prince, the engines of war ground Jerusalem into a city of destruction, just as Daniel was told:

> "Then after the sixty-two weeks the Messiah will be cut off and have nothing, and the people of the prince who is to come will destroy the city and the sanctuary. And its end will come with a flood; even to the end there will be war; desolations are determined." (v. 26)

Let's break this verse down phrase by phrase so we can grasp its meaning more clearly.

"The Messiah will be cut off" refers to Christ's atoning death on the cross. His "hav[ing] nothing" means that, at this time, He has not ushered in His eternal kingdom with power and glory but is waiting in grace for as many as will to come to Him.

"The people of the prince who is to come" foretells the Romans, led by Titus, who "destroy[ed] the city and the sanctuary"—leaving Jerusalem in ruins—in A.D. 70.[4] And, just as the little horn in Daniel 7:23–25 and 8:23–25 has a double fulfillment in Antiochus IV Epiphanes and the Antichrist, so Titus here also prefigures the Antichrist.

The phrase "Its end will come with a flood" paints a picture of judgment rather than prophesying a literal flood.[5] Depending on how the pronoun *its* is translated, this phrase can have a couple of different meanings.

First, *its* could refer to Jerusalem, which was destroyed as judgment for rejecting her Messiah. Israel's flood of sufferings will continue as she endures "war" and "desolations" from the time of Jerusalem's destruction until Christ delivers His people from Gentile dominion.[6]

Or, *its* could actually be the word *his*—"his end will come with a flood"—referring to the Antichrist, who will increase the sorrows and hardships of the Jews in the Tribulation. "His" would connect with the pronoun "he" in the next verse (9:27).

4. J. Dwight Pentecost, "Daniel," in *The Bible Knowledge Commentary*, Old Testament edition, ed. John F. Walvoord and Roy B. Zuck (Wheaton, Ill.: Scripture Press, Victor Books, 1985), p. 1364.

5. R. Laird Harris, Gleason L. Archer, Jr., and Bruce K. Waltke, eds., *Theological Wordbook of the Old Testament* (Chicago, Ill.: Moody Press, 1980), vol. 2, p. 918.

6. Pentecost, "Daniel," p. 1364.

Either way, Daniel, of course, would never have anticipated the long period of time between the sixty-ninth "week" and the seventieth "week." We know this interval as the church age—a time of grace in which "the Gentiles are fellow heirs and fellow members of the body, and fellow partakers of the promise in Christ Jesus through the gospel" (Eph. 3:6). At the Rapture, the church age will end, and Daniel's seventieth "week" will begin. Now let's look at that division of time.

The third division. The seventieth week represents the final chapter of Israel's saga.

> "And he will make a firm covenant with the many for one week, but in the middle of the week he will put a stop to sacrifice and grain offering; and on the wing of abominations will come one who makes desolate, even until a complete destruction, one that is decreed, is poured out on the one who makes desolate." (Dan 9:27)

At the beginning of this seven-year period, the "prince who is to come" of verse 26 will make a peace pact with Israel, permitting them to worship in the restored temple. However, after three and a half years, the wolf will shed his sheep's clothing. He will break his agreement with the Jews, stop the sacrifices in the temple, and set up an abominable religious system with himself in the center (see 7:25; 2 Thess. 2:3–4). For the remaining three and a half years, he will viciously attack the Jews. Jesus issued a serious warning about this period:

> "For then there will be a great tribulation, such as has not occurred since the beginning of the world until now, nor ever shall. And unless those days had been cut short, no life would have been saved; but for the sake of the elect those days shall be cut short." (Matt. 24:21–22)

When all seems lost, though, Christ will deliver a crushing blow to the false prince and his followers. Then, with splendor and majesty, He will inaugurate His kingdom of everlasting righteousness.

The following time line illustrates Daniel's sweeping prophecy.

119

The Seventy Weeks of Daniel 9:24–27

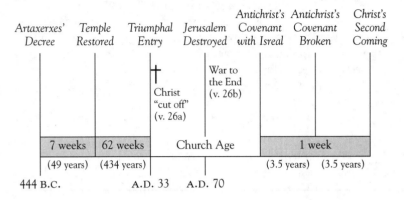

Artaxerxes' Decree	Temple Restored	Triumphal Entry	Jerusalem Destroyed	Antichrist's Covenant with Isreal	Antichrist's Covenant Broken	Christ's Second Coming
		✝ Christ "cut off" (v. 26a)	War to the End (v. 26b)			
7 weeks	62 weeks		Church Age		1 week	
(49 years)	(434 years)				(3.5 years)	(3.5 years)
444 B.C.		A.D. 33	A.D. 70			

The Application

What do we learn from Daniel's incredible prophecy? First, *God is a master of details.* Think of them: the particular number *seventy,* the king's decree, the precise day that Jesus would ride into Jerusalem. They all fall perfectly in line. Can God handle the details in our lives, the ones we worry about so much? You bet He can.

Second, we learn that *God keeps His promises.* These days, a promise isn't worth much unless it's written into a contract drawn up by lawyers and signed in blood. Even then, someone will find a way to break it. God's word, however, is as good as gold. If the Messiah came the first time just as God said He would, we can bank on Him coming again, just as He says He will.

That's a promise we can believe in.

 Living Insights

God's word to Daniel about the exact day of Christ's arrival in Jerusalem is astounding. Let's take a look at a few other messianic prophecies sprinkled throughout the Old Testament. Read the verses listed, and write in the prophecies that Christ fulfills.

Old Testament	New Testament	Fulfilled Prophecy
Isa. 7:14	Matt. 1:18–25	CoNcivu neꝛ A chil₫ & NAmₑD Jesus.

Old Testament	New Testament	Fulfilled Prophecy
Mic. 5:2	Matt. 2:1	HIS BIRTH IN BEthle-ham
Isa. 35:5–6a	Matt. 9:35	would HEAL people
Zech. 9:9	Matt. 21:1–11	KINg will come to you Humbel & REJoice GREATLy. (ou Donkey)
Isa. 53:5	John 19:34	HE WAS Pierceo
Isa. 53:7	Matt. 27:12	HE DiDN'T opeu HiS mouth.
Ps. 22:18	Matt. 27:35	DIVIDEoup His Clothing
Isa. 53:9	Matt. 27:57–60	HE Died we us Aul.

Truly, there is only one response to these incredible prophecies: *awe*. Like the trembling disciples, who said after seeing Jesus calm the storm, "Who then is this, that even the wind and the sea obey Him?" (Mark 4:41), we reply to the Lord, "Who then is this, that even the times and events obey Him?"

Take a moment to express praise to the Lord using Isaiah 46:8–11 as your text of worship. Honor God as One who holds the future, like a stormy sea, in the palm of His hand. Draw near to Him for comfort during these shifting, turbulent times in which we live.

My Praise

_____

_____

_____

_____

_____

Chapter 15

SUPERNATURAL PHENOMENA BETWEEN HEAVEN AND EARTH

Daniel 10

Here's a different way to think about prayer: Whenever we pray, we enter a war zone. Kind of frightening, isn't it? But it's true. Paul, a veteran of spiritual conflict, understood well the spiritual enemies we face:

> Our struggle is not against flesh and blood, but against the rulers, against the powers, against the world forces of this darkness, against the spiritual forces of wickedness in the heavenly places. (Eph. 6:12)

That's why he urged us to arm ourselves, to "stand firm," to pray at all times (vv. 13–18). Daniel 10 provides a window into this invisible battle of heavenly forces and the role prayer plays in it. What you are about to see on the other side may surprise you.

The Time Period and the Prophet

Between the end of Daniel 9 and and the beginning of chapter 10, a history-shaping event occurred in the life of the Jewish nation. In Cyrus' first year as king of Persia, he gave the Jews permission to return to Jerusalem to rebuild the temple (Ezra 1:1–4)—just as Daniel had prayed (Dan. 9:1–19). Israel's captivity was over!

Daniel must have watched the caravans of Jews pulling out of Babylon with tears of joy streaming down his face. After all these years, the exiles were finally going home. How his old heart must have yearned to be young enough to join them.

Now, two years later, "in the third year of Cyrus king of Persia" (10:1), nearly fifty thousand Jews are home and the temple reconstruction is underway. So Daniel's task of praying for his people is through, right? Not at all. Israel's old enemies are harassing the people and sabotaging their plans (Ezra 4:1–5). News of the trouble grieves Daniel, because he knows from his previous visions that more turmoil awaits Israel. And an additional, distressing message confirms this.

We aren't told the specifics of this message, only that it is "one of great conflict" and that Daniel understands it all too well (v. 1). In spite of Israel's present restoration, the nation is destined for more war and bloodshed. But when will this occur? What will bring it about? And how will it end? Weighed down with concern for his people, Daniel turns to the Lord for the missing pieces to this disturbing puzzle.[1]

> In those days I, Daniel, had been mourning for three entire weeks. I did not eat any tasty food, nor did meat or wine enter my mouth, nor did I use any ointment at all, until the entire three weeks were completed. (vv. 2–3)

Day after day, Daniel pleads with God for answers and the heavens are like brass. Can you identify with his struggle? For weeks, maybe months, you've pounded on heaven's door and all you hear is silence from the other side. It can be agonizing.

The Messenger and the Vision

Finally, after twenty-one days of praying, fasting, and grieving, the heavens open up.

> And on the twenty-fourth day of the first month, while I was by the bank of the great river, that is, the Tigris, I lifted my eyes and looked, and behold, there was a certain man dressed in linen, whose waist was girded with a belt of pure gold of Uphaz. His body also was like beryl, his face had the appearance of lightning, his eyes were like flaming torches, his arms and feet like the gleam of polished bronze, and the sound of his words like the sound of a tumult. (vv. 4–6)

Against the black backdrop of unanswered prayer, this brilliant figure flashes out of the sky like a bolt of lightning.

> Now I, Daniel, alone saw the vision, while the men who were with me did not see the vision; nevertheless, a great dread fell on them, and they ran away

---

1. Verse 1 can also be interpreted as an editorial overview of the upcoming passage. If that's the case, the "vision" would refer to the angel Daniel sees in chapter 10; the "message" would be the prophecy the angel gives him in chapters 11 and 12. Verse 2, then, would be Daniel's flashback to the beginning of the account.

to hide themselves. So I was left alone and saw this great vision; yet no strength was left in me, for my natural color turned to a deathly pallor, and I retained no strength. But I heard the sound of his words; and as soon as I heard the sound of his words, I fell into a deep sleep on my face, with my face to the ground. (vv. 7–9)

Although Daniel's companions can't see the angel, they unmistakably sense his presence. Daniel himself turns white, and his body goes limp. We'd say he looked like he'd seen a ghost. But an angel reflecting the light of heaven is much more terrifying than any ghost; and at the sound of this shining being's resounding voice, Daniel faints dead away.[2]

The Prayer and the Response

The next thing Daniel feels is the angel's hand touching him and setting him on his hands and knees (v. 10). Still too weak to move, Daniel steadies himself enough to listen to the angel speak:

And he said to me, "O Daniel, man of high esteem, understand the words that I am about to tell you and stand upright, for I have now been sent to you." And when he had spoken this word to me, I stood up trembling. (v. 11)

The angel will outline a detailed prophecy for Daniel, which is recorded in chapters 11–12. But before unveiling the future, he gives Daniel a fascinating look into the unseen world of good and evil spirits. From this glimpse, we get a firsthand account of the spiritual warfare that rages around us all the time. And we get a deeper understanding of prayer.

The first lesson about prayer and the invisible war is found in verse 12:

Then he said to me, "Do not be afraid, Daniel, for from the first day that you set your heart on understanding this and on humbling yourself before your

---

2. That someone as saintly as Daniel would faint shows us that, no matter how long we've walked with the Lord, we are never prepared to handle the awe of coming face-to-face with heaven's glory.

God, your words were heard, and I have come in response to your words."

From Daniel's first sigh on behalf of his people, God heard every word—a fact that leads us to this principle: *When believers pray, God hears immediately.*

Isn't that encouraging? Nothing can hinder our prayers from reaching God's ear, for He has promised His children immediate access to His throne (see Heb. 4:14–16). But something can hinder His answers from reaching us. Let's listen to what the angel tells Daniel:

> "But the prince of the kingdom of Persia was with-standing [opposing] me for twenty-one days; then behold, Michael, one of the chief princes, came to help me, for I had been left there with the kings of Persia. Now I have come to give you an understanding of what will happen to your people in the latter days, for the vision pertains to the days yet future." (Dan. 10:13–14)

The angel's inside information explains something about prayer we don't often realize: *Demonic forces can delay answers.*

The "prince of the kingdom of Persia" is not a man but a demon—as commentator J. Dwight Pentecost explains.

> God has arranged the angelic realm in differing ranks referred to as "rule, authority, power, and dominion" (Eph. 1:21). Gabriel and Michael have been assigned authority over angels who administer God's affairs for the nation Israel (cf. Michael in Dan. 10:21; 12:1; Jude 9). In imitation Satan has also apparently assigned high-ranking demons to positions of authority over each kingdom. The prince of the Persian kingdom was a satanic representative assigned to Persia.[3]

For twenty-one days (the same period of time that Daniel was praying), this demon commander had God's messenger pinned down

---

3. J. Dwight Pentecost, "Daniel," in *The Bible Knowledge Commentary*, Old Testament edition, ed. John F. Walvoord and Roy B. Zuck (Wheaton, Ill.: Scripture Press, Victor Books, 1985), p. 1366.

until Michael, a higher-ranking angel, could arrive and fend him off.[4]

Remember, this world is enemy territory. We don't know what spiritual forces may be blocking the answers to our prayers. How vital it is that we follow Jesus' command to "pray and not to lose heart" (Luke 18:1), because perseverance in prayer is the key to victory.

How does Daniel respond to the angel's account of heavenly warfare?

> And when he had spoken to me according to these words, I turned my face toward the ground and became speechless. And behold, one who resembled a human being was touching my lips; then I opened my mouth and spoke, and said to him who was standing before me, "O my lord, as a result of the vision anguish has come upon me, and I have retained no strength. For how can such a servant of my lord talk with such as my lord? As for me, there remains just now no strength in me, nor has any breath been left in me." (Dan. 10:15–17)

The angel's struggle, as well as his holy presence, overwhelms Daniel (compare Isaiah's response to God's holiness in Isa. 6:1–7). Also, Daniel's prayers have undoubtedly depleted him physically and emotionally. Deep, serious prayer does that. Our third principle, then, is: *Wrestling in prayer is exhausting work.*

We can't approach the intense fire of God's glory and not feel consumed by the heat. Thankfully, though, God does not abandon us in our weakness.

> Then this one with human appearance touched me again and strengthened me. And he said, "O man of high esteem, do not be afraid. Peace be with you; take courage and be courageous!" Now as soon as he spoke to me, I received strength and said, "May my lord speak, for you have strengthened me." (Dan. 10:18–19)

4. Why didn't God Himself rescue His trapped angel? Gleason L. Archer, Jr. explains, "While God can, of course, override the united resistance of all the forces of hell if he chooses to do so, he accords to demons certain limited powers of obstruction and rebellion somewhat like those he allows humans. In both cases the exercise of free will in opposition to the Lord of heaven is permitted by him when he sees fit." *The Expositor's Bible Commentary,* gen. ed. Frank E. Gaebelein (Grand Rapids, Mich.: Zondervan Publishing House, Regency Reference Library, 1985), vol. 7, p. 125.

When Daniel is at his lowest, feeling unworthy to even raise his head, the angel showers him with grace. He reminds him of his infinite value to God: "O man of high esteem" (see also v. 11). Then, for a third time, the angel reaches down and touches him, strengthening him to receive God's message (see vv. 10, 16). The principle we draw out of Daniel's experience is this: *Following wearisome times in prayer, strength returns in extra measures.*

Did you know that God sometimes gives us strength through the touch of an angel? According to Hebrews 1:14, angels are "ministering spirits, sent out to render service for the sake of those who will inherit salvation." Angels ministered to Christ at certain intense moments in His life, such as after His temptation and in Gethsemane (Matt. 4:11; Luke 22:43). And God still sends angels to encourage His people and protect them against satanic powers.

The passage ends with a final look at the spiritual conflict from the angel's point of view:

> Then he said, "Do you understand why I came to you? But I shall now return to fight against the prince of Persia; so I am going forth, and behold, the prince of Greece is about to come. However, I will tell you what is inscribed in the writing of truth. Yet there is no one who stands firmly with me against these forces except Michael your prince." (Dan. 10:20–21)

These verses flash a sobering warning: *Overcoming demonic forces is not a once-for-all matter.*

The angel must soon return to face not only his old foe but another demon-prince rising out of the west: "the prince of Greece." That's the nature of spiritual warfare. Just when you think you've got a wicked force licked, here it comes again—with another one even stronger. But we don't have to fear. The ultimate victory over Satan is ours, "because greater is He who is in you than he who is in the world" (1 John 4:4).

The Application

It's easy to say, "Don't be afraid," but not so easy to live it when the forces of evil blow like a chill wind across the back of our necks. *Shudder.* It's enough to make the bravest of God's soldiers freeze with fright.

To put courage back in our blood, we need to remember two things: we'd be amazed at the presence of the unseen forces around us (see 2 Kings 6:8–17); and we should be encouraged at the power of the invisible might within us. With Christ as our champion, whom do we fear? The third verse of Martin Luther's stirring hymn, "A Mighty Fortress Is Our God," sums up our confidence in Christ.

> And though this world with devils filled,
> Should threaten to undo us,
> We will not fear, for God hath willed
> His truth to triumph through us.
> The prince of darkness grim,
> We tremble not for him—
> His rage we can endure,
> For lo, his doom is sure:
> One little word shall fell him.[5]

 Living Insights

A policeman hooked on drugs is in danger of losing his job, his family, and his life. . . .

A father awakens after years in a coma to return to the family he realizes he abused and to face his own abusive childhood. . . .

An aging rodeo rider tries to reach out to the son he abandoned and the grandson he never knew, before it's too late. . . .

These are the heartrending situations that Monica and Tess love to handle. Angelic caseworkers on the television show *Touched by an Angel*, the partners travel a celestial Route 66, stepping in and out of people's lives at just the right moment with a word of hope from God.

The charming Monica and Tess are a far cry from the warrior angel Daniel saw. (It's hard to imagine Daniel trembling before an angel named Tess.) But then, all angels don't necessarily look the same. The beings that came to rescue Lot appeared as ordinary men, and they even ate a meal (see Gen. 19:1–3). What do the angels in the following verses look like?

5. Martin Luther, "A Mighty Fortress Is Our God," in *Hymns for the Family of God* (Nashville, Tenn.: Paragon Associates, 1976), no. 118.

Isaiah 6:1–4 _____

_____

Ezekiel 10:9–17 _____

_____

Luke 24:4–5 _____

_____

What else do we know about angels?

- They occupy different seats of power and rank and are vast in number (Col. 1:16; Rev. 5:11).

- They do God's will, thunder His praises, and stand as attendants around His throne (Ps. 103:21; Isa. 6:3–4; Dan. 7:10).

- They have been known to protect God's people from invading armies and release them from prison (2 Kings 6:8–17; Acts 12:7–11).

As children, we were told that God has given us a guardian angel. Is this just a comforting fable? Jesus assures us that it is true: "See that you do not despise one of these little ones, for I say to you, that their angels in heaven continually behold the face of My Father who is in heaven" (Matt. 18:10; see also Ps. 91:11).

Perhaps the most remarkable fact about angels is revealed in Hebrews 13:2. What do you learn about them from that verse?

_____

_____

_____

_____

_____

Although we're warned not to worship angels (Col. 2:18), we can thank the Lord for the spiritual battles they wage on our behalf and the quiet grace they show us. All of us, whether we realize it or not, have been touched by an angel.

Chapter 16

WARS AND
RUMORS OF WAR

Daniel 11

Do not be afraid, O man highly esteemed," the angel encourages Daniel. "Peace! Be strong now; be strong" (Dan. 10:19a NIV). Daniel will surely need all the strength he can muster to keep standing while the angel delivers his apocalyptic message.

In Daniel 11, the angel will draw back the curtain of time, revealing Israel's immediate as well as distant future. Full of betrayal, battles, and bloodshed, the picture promises more heartache for Daniel's people, who are destined to get caught in the crossfire of a world at war.

Wars in the Immediate Future

Continuing his thoughts from chapter 10, the angel recalls another partnership with the archangel Michael. During the first year of Darius the Mede, this divine messenger had come to Michael's aid by arising "to be an encouragement and a protection for him" (11:1; review also 10:13, 21).

God's angels work together to accomplish God's plan—part of which the angel now details vividly for Daniel.[1]

Medo-Persia and Greece

In 11:2 the angel foretells of three kings who will arise after Cyrus and a "fourth [who] will gain far more riches than all of them; . . . he will arouse the whole empire against the realm of Greece." History bears this out: Cyrus was succeeded by Cambyses, Pseudo-Smerdis, Darius I Hystaspes, and then Xerxes (Ahasuerus in the book of Esther). Xerxes—the richest of them all—attacked Greece with a massive army and captured Athens in 480 B.C.

---

1. The historical facts have been gleaned in part from J. Dwight Pentecost, "Daniel," in *The Bible Knowledge Commentary*, Old Testament edition, ed. John F. Walvoord and Roy B. Zuck (Wheaton, Ill.: Scripture Press, Victor Books, 1985), pp. 1367–70; and Leon Wood, *A Commentary on Daniel* (Grand Rapids, Mich.: Zondervan Publishing House, 1973), pp. 280–304.

The "mighty king" who "will rule with great authority and do as he pleases" (v. 3) was Alexander the Great. In verse 4, the angel tolls the bell of his tragic life and legacy: the swift rise to power, the early death, the lack of heirs, the broken empire.

Ruthless infighting among Alexander's generals split the kingdom into four sections. God's message, though, concerns only two of them: Egypt to the south of Israel, grabbed by Ptolemy; and Syria and Babylon to the north, taken by Seleucus.

The Ptolemies and Seleucids

Verses 5–9 predict the tug-of-war between the Ptolemies and Seleucids that ground on for the next hundred years. During this power struggle, the Ptolemies controlled Palestine. Their attempt to make peace is foretold in verse 6. Through marriage to his daughter, Berenice, Ptolemy II offered an alliance to Seleucid's grandson Antiochus II ("the king of the North"). To marry Berenice, Antiochus II had to divorce his wife, Laodice. The scorned Laodice, however, had Berenice murdered; then she lured Antiochus II to remarry her. After the wedding, she poisoned him and put her son, Seleucus II, on the throne.

Verses 7–9 foresee the rest of the story. Berenice's brother ("one of the descendants of her line") avenged her death by attacking Seleucus II ("the king of the North"). He killed Laodice and took back to Egypt "their metal images and their precious vessels of silver and gold." Later, Seleucus II tried to retaliate, but he failed. He "enter[ed] the realm of the king of the South," but "return[ed] to his own land."

Antiochus III the Great

The prophecies in verses 10–19 focus on one of Seleucid II's sons, Antiochus III the Great, who amassed a vast army and drove the Ptolemies out of Palestine (vv. 10–13). He was joined by many Jews—"violent ones among your people" (v. 14)—who viewed him as their champion.

However, Antiochus III the Great wasn't the savior Israel had hoped for. According to the prophecy, he "will do as he pleases," just like Alexander the Great, and

> "no one will be able to withstand him; he will also
> stay for a time in the Beautiful Land, with destruc-
> tion in his hand." (v. 16b)

Verses 17–19 predict Antiochus III's failed attempts to conquer the world. Hoping to establish peace with Egypt, he gave Ptolemy V his daughter, Cleopatra I.[2] Then he launched an invasion into Asia Minor and Greece but was pushed back by Rome's iron legions and forced to pay a heavy tribute. His epitaph in verse 19 sums up his life's disappointing end: "He will stumble and fall and be found no more."

Antiochus IV Epiphanes

Succeeding Antiochus III was his first son, Seleucus IV, who inherited an empty treasury and a heavy debt to Rome. To raise money, he sent his prime minister, Heliodorus, to Jerusalem—"an oppressor through the Jewel of his kingdom" (v. 20)—to seize the temple funds. Seleucus IV was later murdered by this power-hungry prime minister.

The dead king's brother took "the kingdom by intrigue" (v. 21), stealing the throne from his nephew and the rightful heir, Demetrius Soter. We know this usurper as the little horn from Daniel 8:9–13, the harbinger of the Antichrist: Antiochus IV Epiphanes. His treacheries in Israel began when he removed the pious and respected high priest Onias III, "the prince of the covenant" (11:22).

Elsewhere, Antiochus IV played a shrewd game of politics. With deceptive promises, he lured the king of Egypt into an alliance (v. 23) and accomplished "what his fathers never did"—he redistributed the wealth and won widespread support among the lower classes (v. 24).

When he became strong, he invaded Egypt and defeated Ptolemy VI (v. 25). After the battle, the two kings feasted together, toasting and making bargains. But both were deceitful (v. 27). As a result, Antiochus IV failed to take control of Egypt.

Frustrated at only a partial victory, Antiochus IV returned to his land but, on the way, took out his aggression on the Jews. Setting his heart "against the holy covenant" (v. 28), he wreaked havoc in temple affairs, set up his pawn as high priest, and cruelly crushed a minor rebellion.

Two years later, in 168 B.C., he tried to conquer Egypt again. However, Roman "ships of Kittim" (i.e. Cyprus) met him in the

---

2. The most famous Cleopatra, who dallied with Julius Caesar and Mark Antony, lived much later—from 69 to 30 B.C. *Encyclopaedia Britannica*, 15th ed., see "Cleopatra 4."

Egyptian harbor, and a Roman emissary warned him to withdraw—or else (v. 30a).[3] Humiliated, Antiochus IV did an about-face and returned through Palestine. He vented his rage on the Jews once more, this time slaughtering thousands, outlawing Judaism, and converting the temple into a pagan shrine (vv. 30b–31).

This was a dark period in Israel's history. Finally, a light of hope flickered when the Maccabean family launched a revolt against Antiochus IV (v. 32). Many courageous Jews lost their lives during the rebellion (vv. 33–35), falling "by sword and by flame, by captivity and by plunder, for many days" (v. 33). Finally, in 165 B.C., Judas Maccabaeus cleansed the temple and restored worship. But this wasn't the end of religious persecution for the Jews; trouble would follow God's people through the years, all the way to "the end time" (v. 35b).

The Final War in the Distant Future

Having laid out Israel's immediate future, the angel now lifts his gaze to the distant future, using Antiochus IV as a bridge from the near to the far.

> "Then the king will do as he pleases, and he will exalt and magnify himself above every god, and will speak monstrous things against the God of gods; and he will prosper until the indignation is finished, for that which is decreed will be done." (v. 36)

As the passage develops, Antiochus fades and the prophecies zoom in on the Antichrist.

The Antichrist's Style

From previous studies, we know that the Antichrist will make a peace agreement with Israel during the first half of the Tribulation. At the midpoint, he will break that treaty and set up his abominable self-religion in Jerusalem (see 9:27; 2 Thess. 2:3–4; Rev. 13:1–8). The angel centers here on that event and on the cataclysmic three-and-a-half years that will follow.

> "And he will show no regard for the gods of his

---

3. "Popillius Laenas took to Antiochus a letter forbidding him to engage in war with Egypt. When Antiochus asked for time to consider, the emissary drew a circle in the sand around Antiochus and demanded that he give his answer before he stepped out of the circle." Pentecost, "Daniel," *Bible Knowledge Commentary*, pp. 1369–70.

fathers or for the desire of women,[4] nor will he show
regard for any other god; for he will magnify himself
above them all." (Dan. 11:37)

Proud to an extreme, the Antichrist will toss aside all other
religions and demand that the nations worship him alone. No person or thing will be his lord. Instead, he will recognize only the
god of war, and he will honor "him" by spending the wealth of his
treasuries building up his vast army (v. 38). With his coalition of
western nations and huge arsenal, the Antichrist will begin to
expand his dominion. A "foreign god"—Satan—will help him battle "the strongest of fortresses" (v. 39a). He will also

> "give great honor to those who acknowledge him,
> and he will cause them to rule over the many, and
> will parcel out land for a price." (v. 39b)

Controlling great expanses of land, the Antichrist will grant
some to his loyal followers for favors rendered, and this will gain
him a large following.

The Antichrist's Strategy

Two other world powers, though, will unite to overthrow the
Antichrist in a two-pronged assault against the heart of his
empire—Israel.

> "And at the end time the king of the South will
> collide with him, and the king of the North will
> storm against him with chariots, with horsemen, and
> with many ships." (v. 40a)

The southern power most likely will be an Egypt-based Arabian
confederation; the northern power, Russia.[5] Like freight trains on
a collision course, these two great coalitions will converge on Israel
in an explosion of force. The Russians will fail to capture the
Antichrist, but they will

> "enter the Beautiful Land, and many countries will

---

4. Some have interpreted this statement to mean that the Antichrist will be homosexual.
Or perhaps it simply means that sexual desires won't master him.

5. Ezekiel talked about this northern king as "Gog of the land of Magog, the prince of Rosh,
Meshech, and Tubal" (Ezek. 38:2). According to verses 14–16, he will sweep "out of the
remote parts of the north" to attack Israel (v. 15).

fall; but these will be rescued out of his hand: Edom, Moab and the foremost of the sons of Ammon."[6] (v. 41)

Then the northern leader will "stretch out his hand against other countries, and the land of Egypt will not escape" (v. 42a). He will double-cross the Arabian confederation, and with a full head of steam, his powerful army will plow through northeast Africa.

> "But he will gain control over the hidden treasures of gold and silver, and over all the precious things of Egypt; and Libyans and Ethiopians will follow at his heels." (v. 43)

Glorying in his victories, the king of the north will hear "rumors from the East and from the North" (v. 44a), probably regarding a counterattack. He will regroup his armies and

> "go forth with great wrath to destroy and annihilate many. And he will pitch the tents of his royal pavilion between the seas and the beautiful Holy Mountain." (vv. 44b–45a)

No doubt, he will make his final stand on the plain of Megiddo, or Jezreel, in the center of Israel. As the hordes from the east (probably China) and the Antichrist's forces from the west descend on Israel, the stage will be set for the final conflict—the battle of Armageddon (see Rev. 16:12–16).

What happens next can hardly be described. Although the angel simply says that the king of the north "will come to his end, and no one will help him" (Dan. 11:45b), Ezekiel foretells a mighty earthquake and "a torrential rain, with hailstones, fire, and brimstone" (Ezek. 38:22; see also vv. 19–23). Some see this as the frightening effects of nuclear warfare. At any rate, the Russian armies will be wiped out, leaving the forces of east and west to clash, while God pours out His righteous judgment on the world (see Rev. 16:17–21).

---

6. The pronoun *he* in verses 40–45 could refer to the "king of the North" according to James Montgomery Boice, *The Last and Future World* (Grand Rapids, Mich.: Zondervan Publishing House, 1974), pp. 109–11. Or it could refer to the Antichrist, per Pentecost, "Daniel," *Bible Knowledge Commentary*, p. 1372.

What Does It All Mean for Today?

Whew! The prophecies in Daniel 11 take our breath away. Hundreds of years of history flash before our eyes with the same recurring story: nation rises against nation, sword strikes against sword. Is there any hope in this tale of death and destruction?

Peter has an answer for us:

> The Lord is not slow about His promise, as some count slowness, but is patient toward you, not wishing for any to perish but for all to come to repentance. (2 Pet. 3:9)

Christ offers His hand of salvation to everyone. As long as one more sinner will come to Him, Christ will hold back His judgment. Could it be that your unsaved neighbor or husband or wife or child is that one person Christ is waiting for? Won't you show him or her the way of salvation today?

Living Insights

The detail in Daniel 11 is amazing. Not only do we see kingdoms rising and falling, we see actual people and events portrayed so precisely that some Bible scholars can't believe the prophecies were written beforehand.

Yet, as Isaiah wrote,

> "I am God, and there is no one like Me,
> Declaring the end from the beginning
> And from ancient times things which have not
>   been done,
> Saying, 'My purpose will be established,
> And I will accomplish all My good pleasure.'"
> (Isa. 46:9b–10)

But God doesn't want us to merely admire His handiwork. He wants us to be changed by it.

What does God's precision in the past tell you about the prophecies that are yet to be fulfilled?

_____

_____

How does knowing the future change the way you live in the present, concerning . . .

• your unsaved friends and family members _____

_____

• your priorities _____

_____

• how you view your problems _____

_____

The next time you hear of "wars and rumors of wars," think of the prophecies in Daniel. And pray for God's strength to live for Him, no matter what the future holds.

Chapter 17

A PROPHETIC QUARTET

Daniel 12:1–4

Oklahoma City, April 19, 1995, 9:02 A.M. A stomach-churning rumble throbbed for miles around when a moving van loaded with explosives detonated in front of the Alfred P. Murrah Federal Office Building. The blast sheared off the face of the structure, causing an avalanche of concrete. Windows blew out of buildings as far as a mile away. A fireball roared down the street, blackening everything in its path.

In the Murrah building, an eerie mosaic of instant death and inexplicable escape materialized through the rubble. One young woman

> was sitting at her desk beside a co-worker when the bomb exploded. She threw her hands over her face, was propelled to the back wall in her wheeled desk chair and survived. Her deskmate apparently grabbed for something solid and rode it down eight floors to his death.[1]

Less than a week earlier, laughter and childish exuberance had filled the building's daycare Easter party. On this day, there was only appalling silence. On this day, a young boy lay in a temporary morgue; a little red-haired girl, in intensive care.

All told, 168 people died, nineteen of them children.[2]

None of these people could have known that something so horrendous was coming. They were helpless to stop it, helpless to save themselves.

Daniel, as we saw in the previous chapter, did foresee the great agony that would descend on his people. But seeing it didn't make him any less helpless than those in Oklahoma City. Rather, it probably intensified his dread of what was coming.

If the angel's message had ended there, Daniel would have despaired. But when chapter 12 opens, the apocalypse fades and

---

1. Mike Brake, "Building a Book of Tears," Chronicle, *Writer's Digest*, March 1996, p. 72.

2. Jesse Katz, "Kids Put Blast Behind Them in Tiny Steps," *Los Angeles Times*, April 19, 1996, sec. A, p. 10.

deliverance shines bright and strong. As the Oklahoma rescue workers were the light of hope for every trapped person, so Israel's guardian, the archangel Michael, would be a beacon of life to every one of Daniel's people pinned in the wreckage of human history.

Setting and Background

Continuing the message to Daniel he began in chapter 10, the angel now lifts the veil of the future to reveal God's delivering hand.

> "Now at that time Michael, the great prince who stands guard over the sons of your people, will arise. And there will be a time of distress such as never occurred since there was a nation until that time; and at that time your people, everyone who is found written in the book, will be rescued." (12:1)

The "time" the angel keeps referring to is not just the seven-year Tribulation; it is a period of intense persecution coming midway through it, known as the Great Tribulation (see Matt. 24:21). This time will come at the halfway point of the seventieth week (Dan. 9:27), after the Antichrist sets up his "abomination of desolation" in the temple (see Matt. 24:15). For these three-and-a-half years, the Jews will endure a specialized, satanic persecution that will funnel into the final world war.[3]

Though the Jews have endured torture and death throughout history, they have never experienced a holocaust like the one that's coming.

Thankfully, as the angel assures Daniel, Michael will arise with God's deliverance in hand.

People and Events

From the angel's words in Daniel 12:1 and the verses that follow, four types of people emerge. Let's get acquainted with each and see what we can learn from them.

---

3. This persecution will fulfill Jesus' prophecy about the Jews being "trampled under foot by the Gentiles until the times of the Gentiles be fulfilled" (Luke 21:24). It will also bring to an end God's setting aside and "partial hardening" of the Jews as a result of their rejection of Christ (see Rom. 11:1–25).

Those Whose Names Are Written in the Book

In verse 1, the angel has told Daniel that "at that time your people, everyone who is found written in the book, will be rescued." What book is this? Most likely, God's book of life. God has recorded the names of everyone He has redeemed since time began (see Luke 10:20; Phil. 4:3; Rev. 3:5; 13:8; 17:8; 20:12, 15; 21:27). Adam's name is etched in the book; so is Noah's, Abraham's, Esther's, David's . . . and ours, too, if Christ is our Savior.

What an encouragement for the Jews who turn to Christ during the Tribulation. God has promised to preserve this special remnant and usher them into the millennial kingdom—the messianic rule they have dreamed of for centuries (see Zech. 14:9–11). No more terror. No more dread. Christ will reign over the earth in perfect peace and righteousness, and God's elect who survive the Tribulation will become the first generation in His new world.

Those Who Die during the Tribulation

What about those who die in the Tribulation? What will be their fate?

> "And many of those who sleep in the dust of the ground
> will awake, these to everlasting life, but the others
> to disgrace and everlasting contempt." (Dan. 12:2)

As if stirring them from a nightmarish sleep, God will wake those who have died, resurrecting them for judgment. Looking through the lens of the New Testament, we can see two resurrections in Daniel 12:2. The first will occur at the end of the Tribulation, when the redeemed will be raised "to everlasting life." Revelation 20:4–6 pictures this for us.

> And I saw thrones, and they sat upon them, and judgment was given to them. And I saw the souls of those who had been beheaded because of the testimony of Jesus and because of the word of God, and those who had not worshiped the beast or his image, and had not received the mark upon their forehead and upon their hand; and they came to life and reigned with Christ for a thousand years. The rest of the dead did not come to life until the thousand years were completed. This is the first resurrection. Blessed and holy is the one who has a part in

the first resurrection; over these the second death has no power, but they will be priests of God and of Christ and will reign with Him for a thousand years.

The second will occur at the end of the Millennium, when the unredeemed will be raised "to disgrace and everlasting contempt" (Dan. 12:2), which Revelation 20:11–15 describes in terrifying detail.

And I saw a great white throne and Him who sat upon it, from whose presence earth and heaven fled away, and no place was found for them. And I saw the dead, the great and the small, standing before the throne, and books were opened; and another book was opened, which is the book of life; and the dead were judged from the things which were written in the books, according to their deeds. And the sea gave up the dead which were in it, and death and Hades gave up the dead that were in them; and they were judged, every one of them according to their deeds. And death and Hades were thrown into the lake of fire. This is the second death, the lake of fire. And if anyone's name was not found written in the book of life, he was thrown into the lake of fire.

The chart on the next page explains Scripture's overall teaching on bodily resurrection.

Those Who Have Insight

Daniel 12:3a describes a third group of people—"those who have insight," or "the instructors" (NASB margin). This group certainly includes those who will teach the Scriptures during the Tribulation, those new believers God anoints with insight into His Word so they can build up fellow believers. But the idea extends beyond that, as C. F. Keil makes clear. Referring back to Daniel 11:33–35, the word *insight*

is here, as there, not limited to the teachers, but denotes the intelligent [or *wise*, NIV] who, by instructing their contemporaries by means of word and deed, have awakened them to steadfastness and fidelity to their confession in the times of tribulation and have strengthened their faith, and some of whom have in

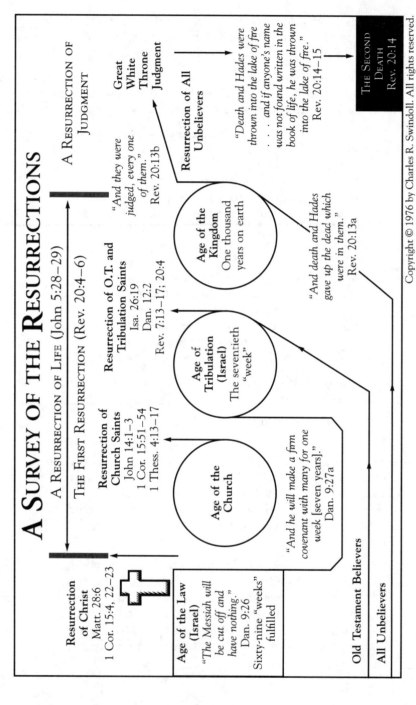

A Survey of the Resurrections

A Resurrection of Life (John 5:28–29)

A Resurrection of Judgment

The First Resurrection (Rev. 20:4–6)

Resurrection of Christ
Matt. 28:6
1 Cor. 15:4, 22–23

Resurrection of Church Saints
John 14:1–3
1 Cor. 15:51–54
1 Thess. 4:13–17

Resurrection of O.T. and Tribulation Saints
Isa. 26:19
Dan. 12:2
Rev. 7:13–17; 20:4

Great White Throne Judgment

"And they were judged, every one of them."
Rev. 20:13b

Resurrection of All Unbelievers

"Death and Hades were thrown into the lake of fire . . . and if anyone's name was not found written in the book of life, he was thrown into the lake of fire."
Rev. 20:14–15

The Second Death
Rev. 20:14

Age of the Church

Age of Tribulation (Israel)
The seventieth "week"

Age of the Kingdom
One thousand years on earth

"And death and Hades gave up the dead which were in them."
Rev. 20:13a

Age of the Law (Israel)
"The Messiah will be cut off and have nothing."
Dan. 9:26
Sixty-nine "weeks" fulfilled

"And he will make a firm covenant with many for one week [seven years]."
Dan. 9:27a

Old Testament Believers

All Unbelievers

142

war sealed their testimony with their blood.[4]

God promises a bright future for these wise people, whose lives will instruct others in the faith: they "will shine brightly like the brightness of the expanse of heaven" (12:3a). Or as Jesus put it, referring to this passage from Daniel, "The righteous will shine forth as the sun in the kingdom of their Father" (Matt. 13:43). God will reward His faithful people, bestowing His own imperishable, everlasting glory on them (compare Isa. 60:1–3; and Matt. 17:2 with 1 John 3:2).

Those Who Lead the Many to Righteousness

"Those who lead the many to righteousness" form the fourth group (Dan. 12:3b). They are the evangelists in the Tribulation, the courageous ones who will risk their lives to lead others to Christ. Many of them will be martyred for their outspoken faith, their bodies burned and tossed on refuse heaps. The world will forget them, but not God (see 1 Cor. 15:58; Heb. 6:10). To Him, they will be "like the stars forever and ever" (Dan. 12:3b).

Words and Knowledge

The angel wraps up his message to Daniel with a closing command:

> "But as for you, Daniel, conceal these words and seal
> up the book until the end of time; many will go back
> and forth, and knowledge will increase." (v. 4)

Why would God hide His prophetic message? Gleason Archer explains that, in this context, *conceal* and *seal* have a different meaning than we might expect.

> In the ancient Near East, important documents such
> as contracts, promissory notes, and deeds of convey-
> ance were written out in duplicate. The original
> document was kept in a secure repository, safe
> ("closed up" [NIV]) from later tampering. . . .

---

4. C. F. Keil, *Biblical Commentary on the Book of Daniel*, trans. M. G. Easton (Grand Rapids, Mich.: William B. Eerdmans Publishing Co., 1959), p. 483. See also Gleason L. Archer, Jr., "Daniel," in *The Expositor's Bible Commentary*, gen. ed. Frank E. Gaebelein (Grand Rapids, Mich.: Zondervan Publishing House, Regency Reference Library, 1985), vol. 7, p. 152.

Though copies might be made from it, the original was to remain secure so that it might be consulted if any future challenge of its terms were made.

The practice of "sealing" was likewise derived from Near Eastern usage. . . . First of all came the seal of the recording scribe himself, who in this case was Daniel, and then the seals of the various witnesses who heard the exact words as they were dictated to the scribe. Once the document was thus sealed, it became the official and unchangeable text. . . . Daniel, then, was to certify by his personal seal, as it were, to the faithfulness of the foregoing text as an exact transcript of what God had communicated to him through his angel. Thus the record would be preserved unaltered down to the day when all the predictions would be fulfilled.[5]

The phrase "many will go back and forth, and knowledge will increase" simply means that Daniel's contemporaries won't be able to grasp the entire message. But as history unfolds, and in light of John's Revelation, the prophecy will become clearer—especially to those who dig diligently for the meaning.

Summary and Relevance

What insights do we discover from this section of Daniel's book? First, *the world honors the famous and soon forgets them; God honors the unknown and never forgets them.* Sports heroes and movie stars may sparkle against the night sky like fireworks, but all too often they burn out and drift away, forgotten ashes. God's heroes, however, may not flash in the world's eyes, but God sees them. He's inscribed their names in His book, and they will be remembered forever.

Second, *the world gives its rewards now; God saves His until later.* Most people don't notice if we share the little we have with those who have less or take the time to show God's love to the unlovely. But God does. And heaven's rewards are far brighter than any temporal trophies we might receive on earth.

Third, *the world's methods are always connected with time; God's*

---

5. Archer, "Daniel," pp. 153–54. This is similar to what John said at the close of Revelation (see 22:18–19).

are always connected with eternity. An investment in a blue-chip stock may yield dividends for years to come, but an investment in your spiritual life will draw an eternal payoff. And the best part about this investment? It's guaranteed!

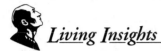
Living Insights

An aging missionary couple sailed home to England after forty years of foreign service. Aboard the same ship was the Queen of England, who was returning after a royal visit abroad. At the harbor, she was greeted with a grand reception—a band trumpeted her arrival, cameras flashed, enthusiastic crowds cheered and whooped at the sight of their queen. Watching the spectacle from a distance, the husband mumbled, "We've been laboring all these years for the Lord, yet this woman merely inherited a throne and half the country turns out to honor her." Gently, his wife touched his shoulder and reminded him, "But dear, we're not home yet."[6]

All of us need that gentle touch on the shoulder from time to time, don't we? God saves His rewards until later, when we sail into our final port. Waiting for that day isn't easy, though, particularly when we see the world's glittering treasures paraded before us.

How are you doing in the struggle to hold on to that eternal perspective against tempting short-term gratification?

_____

_____

_____

In our passage, God encourages us to look to the heavens (see Dan. 12:3). Like the bright expanse in our night sky, God's galaxy shimmers with faithful servants who may have been discarded on earth but are now shining lights in heaven.

What further encouragement do these verses offer?

1 Corinthians 15:50–58 _____

_____

6. Adapted from Ray C. Stedman in *Jesus Teaches on Prayer* (Waco, Tex.: Word Books; Palo Alto, Calif.: Discovery Foundation, 1975), pp. 30–31.

2 Corinthians 4:16–18 _____

_____

Galatians 6:9 _____

_____

Colossians 3:1–4 _____

_____

In what ways can an eternal perspective help you in the following areas:

• coping with a specific hardship or disappointment?

_____

_____

• persevering in a certain ministry?

_____

_____

• loosening your grip on something you own?

_____

_____

The next time the world rolls out the red carpet for one of its celebrities, remind yourself, "I'm not home yet." And try to imagine the cheers and whoops you'll receive the moment you step into heaven.

Chapter 18

THE END OF THE AGE
Daniel 12:5–13

W hen Daniel began his vigil for Israel on the banks of the Tigris river (Dan. 10:4), little did he realize that his prayers would set him on such a long prophetic journey. As the prophecy concludes (12:4), he finds himself where he started. The rippling river, the gentle wind, and the swaying trees bring him back to the present.

The prophecy is over . . . but the story isn't. There remains one more scene before the curtain falls—one more opportunity for Daniel, and us, to marvel at God's amazing plan for the end of the age.

Expository Explanation

We can best appreciate this final section by examining its three major elements: the individuals involved, the questions asked, and the answers given.

Individuals Involved

As the scene unfolds, Daniel is listening to the last words of the prophecy when he realizes he's not alone:

> Then I, Daniel, looked and behold, two others
> were standing, one on this bank of the river, and
> the other on that bank of the river. (v. 5)

These angels, drawn by an inner longing to look into the things of God (see 1 Pet. 1:12), have been listening eagerly to the prophecy too. Like us, they want to know what God has in store for the end of the world.

Now there are four individuals by the river: Daniel, the two new angels, and "the man dressed in linen" (Dan. 12:6)—the mighty angel we first met in chapter 10 (vv. 5–6).[1]

---

1. Since "the man dressed in linen" looks more majestic and powerful than the other angels, some conclude that he is an appearance of Christ (compare Dan. 10:5–6 with Rev. 1:12–16). But Christ could not be thwarted by a demon (Dan. 10:13), so those who hold this view see an additional angel in chapter 10—one who is sent by Christ, fights the demon, touches Daniel, and delivers the prophecy (10:10–21). See J. Vernon McGee, *Daniel* (Pasadena, Calif.: Thru the Bible Books, 1978), pp. 163–66, 198.

Questions Asked

In the verses that follow, two questions emerge—the first, from angelic lips.

> And one said to the man dressed in linen, who was above the waters of the river, "How long will it be until the end of these wonders?" (12:6)

Daniel, whose mind is still spinning from the prophecy, later raises a second question:

> As for me, I heard but could not understand; so I said, "My lord, what will be the outcome of these events?" (v. 8)

While the angel focuses on the timing of God's judgment, Daniel is concerned about the results. Let's see how the hovering angel responds to these two questions.

Answers Given

He answers the first question with an oath:

> And [Daniel] heard the man dressed in linen, who was above the waters of the river, as he raised his right hand and his left toward heaven, and swore by Him who lives forever that it would be for a time, times, and half a time; and as soon as they finish shattering the power of the holy people, all these events will be completed. (v. 7)

"Time, times, and half a time" refers to years. One year, two years, and half a year equals three and a half years (see 7:25). The angel has in mind the second, horrible half of the Tribulation— the seventieth "week"—after the Antichrist breaks his peace covenant and sets up his religious headquarters in Jerusalem (9:27). For three and a half years, he will persecute Israel, shattering God's precious vessels of faith with his fists of iron (7:21–25; 8:24). Jesus called this nightmare the "great tribulation" and assured that "unless those days had been cut short, no life would have been saved" (Matt. 24:21–22).

Raising both hands toward heaven,[2] the angel makes a solemn

---

2. Raising one hand was sufficient to take an oath (see Deut. 32:40). The angel doubly affirmed the truth of his message by raising both hands.

pledge that what God has promised will come true. At the darkest hour, when the persecution of the saints has reached its peak, God will cry out, "Enough!" The clouds will part, and Christ will charge down from heaven to deal the beast a crushing blow (Dan. 11:45; Rev. 19:11–21).

The angel tells us more about this three-and-a-half-year period in Daniel 12:11:

> "And from the time that the regular sacrifice is abol-
> ished, and the abomination of desolation is set up,
> there will be 1,290 days."

According to the Jewish calendar, three and a half years totals only 1,260 days. So why does the angel add thirty days to make 1,290? One possible reason is the massacre at the battle of Armageddon will be so extensive that it will take another thirty days to clean up afterward (see Rev. 14:17–20).

Interestingly, the angel adds forty-five more days in Daniel 12:12,

> "How blessed is he who keeps waiting and attains
> to the 1,335 days!"

Although we can't be sure, the purpose of the additional forty-five days may be twofold: (1) to allow time for Christ to judge the Jews and Gentiles after the Tribulation (see "A Survey of the Judgments" chart at the end of this chapter),[3] and (2) to provide Him time to set up the government for His millennial reign on earth. In the age to come, His faithful followers will hold privileged positions of power, ruling and reigning with Him (see 7:27).

The angel responds to Daniel's question about what the outcome will be with a less direct answer.

> And he said, "Go your way, Daniel, for these words
> are concealed and sealed up until the end time.
> Many will be purged, purified and refined; but the
> wicked will act wickedly, and none of the wicked
> will understand, but those who have insight will
> understand." (12:9–10)

Sensing Daniel's concern for his people, the angel tells him not

---

3. For more information about these end-times judgments, see J. Dwight Pentecost's chapter, "The Judgments Associated with the Second Advent" in *Things to Come: A Study in Biblical Eschatology* (Grand Rapids, Mich.: Zondervan Publishing House, Academie Books, 1958), pp. 412–26.

to worry, the fulfillment of these prophecies is far in the future. That's why he should preserve them—conceal and seal them—until the end of time (compare Rev. 22:10).

In the meantime, good people will get better, and the bad will get worse. God's people will be "purged, purified and refined"—made ready to welcome the coming of the King of Kings. The wicked, however, will sink deeper into darkness, oblivious to the judgment they are storing up for themselves (Rom. 2:5).

In the last verse of Daniel, the angel adds a personal note to the highly esteemed prophet:

> "But as for you, go your way to the end; then you will enter into rest and rise again for your allotted portion at the end of the age." (Dan. 12:13)

He's essentially saying, "Carry on to the end of life, Daniel. Don't let visions of the future hinder your walk with the Lord today."

That's good advice for believers of any time. Too much weight on prophecy can tip anybody over the edge of good sense. Some of the Thessalonian Christians, for example, got so caught up in prophecy that they quit their jobs to wait for the coming of Christ. Paul had to tell them to get back to work and eat their own bread, because they were becoming a burden on everyone else (2 Thess. 3:10–15).

The best advice is *stay balanced.* Look forward to the future, but keep your feet in the present.

Concluding Counsel

As the curtain closes on our study of Daniel, we are invited to take three thoughts with us. First, *the more time we spend with God, the more teachable we become.* The most impressive image in the book is not the fiery furnace or the giant statue or even the fantastic visions. It's the picture of Daniel on his knees before God day after day, year after year. In the midst of turbulent times, he was continually praying, "Lord, speak to me, show me Your way, keep me faithful." This open attitude attuned his life toward God and made him ready to receive the messages God had for him.

Second, *the more questions we ask God, the more dependent we become on Him.* Daniel wasn't afraid to ask questions when he didn't understand a vision or dream. He didn't try to solve God's divine puzzles on his own. Instead, he looked to the Source of all truth for answers.

Third, *the more truth we discover about God, the more profound He becomes to us.* Seeing God through the book of Daniel is like peering into the night sky through a telescope. The book takes us beyond a naked-eye knowledge about Him and opens whole new worlds of understanding. We see the starry wonder and detail of His prophetic plan. We discover galaxies of His power we never knew existed. The more we learn, the more we realize how much we don't know. As we marvel at the vastness of His presence, our mouths fall silent. Debates fade. Knees bow in worship.

The awe of God—that is the greatest lesson Daniel's book teaches us. From the words of the once-proud king Nebuchadnezzar, our praise resounds:

> "How great are His signs,
> And how mighty are His wonders!
> His kingdom is an everlasting kingdom,
> And His dominion is from generation to
>   generation." (Dan. 4:3)

 Living Insights

The two questions posed in this passage emerge from the angel's grim announcement in verse 1:

> And there will be a time of distress such as never
> occurred since there was a nation until that time.

For anyone enduring a time of distress, those questions flow like tears: *How long will the pain last, Lord? And what's the outcome—what's going to come of all this?*

We can summarize the angel's first answer this way: "For a time."

It's not blind optimism to believe that things will get better, that sorrow is only for a time. Life is full of changing seasons. Take a look at the many "times" in Ecclesiastes 3:1–8.

What about those with chronic illnesses and disabilities? Even for them, there will be a time to heal and dance, when they see Christ face-to-face. No Christian's dark night lasts forever (see Ps. 30:5b).

The angel doesn't really provide an answer for our second question, What's going to come of all this? He only gives a command—"Go your way." Similarly, God doesn't always tell us the reasons for our hard times or even what good will come of them. We simply have to trust Him and keep going.

Can you trust the Lord, even when He doesn't answer your questions?

Of Daniel's many qualities, one of his strongest was his ability to stay close to God in good times and bad. But you may say, "How can I stay close to God when I can't see or feel Him?" That's where faith comes in—faith not in a creed or a force but in a Person. The more you spend time with God and get to know Him as a person, the more you will want to stay close to Him. That was Daniel's secret of strength. May it become your key to spiritual strength as well.

 ## Digging Deeper

To help anchor in your mind the truths from the final six chapters of Daniel, take some time for a brief review.

In chapters 1–6, we saw how the historical events in Daniel's life revealed God's sovereign hand. That same divine influence has been at work in Daniel's prophetic dreams and visions in chapters 7–12. See if you can trace this theme through the last half of the book.

CHAPTER 7: How does Daniel's vision of the four beasts show God and the kingdom of His Son as more powerful than the kingdoms of the earth? (Clue: see especially vv. 9–14, 25–27.)

_____

_____

_____

CHAPTER 8: In the vision of the ram and the goat, what gets broken in verses 7, 8, and 25? Why is that recurring theme important in this prophecy?

_____

_____

_____

CHAPTER 9: In his prayer of confession, Daniel expresses spiritual and emotional brokenness before God. Why do you think that attitude especially pleases the Lord?

_____

_____

_____

Why do you think the prophecy of the seventy weeks is considered the backbone of biblical prophecy (vv. 24–27)?

_____

_____

_____

CHAPTER 10: Based on Daniel's experience, what role do our prayers play in the spiritual battles waged all around us?

_____

_____

_____

CHAPTER 11: This prophecy reaches a crescendo in the final conflict between the forces of good and evil in verses 40–45. How does this prophecy confirm the sovereignty of God?

_____

_____

_____

CHAPTER 12: The book of Daniel concludes with the grand finale of God's redemptive plan for the world—our resurrection and God's judgment of saints and sinners (vv. 1–2). How does this hope give you faith in God and in His providential hand in the affairs of the world?

_____

_____

_____

A SURVEY OF THE JUDGMENTS

Name	Subjects	Time	Place	Basis	Results
The Cross	Satan judged *John 16:11* Sin judged *Rom. 6:6–10; 8:1–4*	A.D. 30 (traditional) or A.D. 33[1]	Calvary	Finished work of Christ	Death of Christ, Satan doomed, sin overthrown, sinners justified
Self-judgment of believers	Christians in the church age who sin *1 Cor. 11:27–31* *1 John 1:9*	Present time	Earth	Blood of Christ	Immediate forgiveness, permanent removal of confessed sin
Divine discipline	Believers who neglect the confession of sin *Heb. 12:6* *1 John 1:5–10*	Present time	Earth	God's love, scriptural warning	Suffering and misery until confession of sin . . . perhaps even death
Judgment seat of Christ	Believers taken at the Rapture of the church *2 Cor. 5:10* *1 Cor. 3:10–15*	Immediately after the Rapture of the church	Presence of the Lord	Works performed during earthly life	Either rewards or the loss of rewards (crowns)

Name	Subjects	Time	Place	Basis	Results
Living Jews	Unbelieving Jews alive at the end of Tribulation *Matt. 25:1–30*	At Second Advent	Earth	Their works (separating saved Israel from unsaved)	Unsaved are cast off into judgment; saved enter the kingdom
Living Gentiles (sheep/goats)	Unbelieving Gentiles alive at the end of the Tribulation *Joel 3:1–2* *Matt. 25:31–46*	Following the judgment of the living Jews	Earth	Treatment of saved Israel— "Brothers of Mine"—during Tribulation *Matt. 25:40*	Unsaved face eternal judgment; saved enter the kingdom
Fallen angels	Angels being held captive *2 Pet. 2:4* *Jude 6*	After the kingdom age (?)	Angelic realm	Their decision to follow Satan when he fell	Sent to permanent place of punishment
Great White Throne	All unbelievers (physically and spiritually dead) *Rev. 20:11–15*	After the earth is judged by fire *2 Pet. 3:7–10*	Between heaven and earth—in space	Worthless works of the unsaved	Eternal separation from God— "second death"

1. Harold W. Hoehner, *Chronological Aspects of the Life of Christ* (Grand Rapids, Mich.: Zondervan Publishing House, Acadamie Books, 1977), p. 114.

BOOKS FOR
PROBING FURTHER

Daniel—his book is so much more than stories of fiery furnaces and lions' dens, isn't it? It's a reaffirmation of God's authority, sovereignty, and supremacy over Jew and Gentile, believer and unbeliever alike.

The Lord is king. He remembers His people. He honors those who trust Him. He will bring evil to an end. . . . These are a few of the rich themes Daniel has put in our hands and our hearts—you've probably discovered quite a few more along the way. To help you continue exploring the book of Daniel and topics that spring from it, we recommend the following books.

Conyers, A. J. *The End: What Jesus Really Said about the Last Things.* Downers Grove, Ill.: InterVarsity Press, 1995.

Foster, Richard J. *Prayer: Finding the Heart's True Home.* San Francisco, Calif.: HarperSanFrancisco, 1992.

Jeremiah, David, with C. C. Carlson. *The Handwriting on the Wall: Secrets from the Prophecies of Daniel.* Dallas, Tex.: Word Publishing, 1992. Expositional commentary.

Pentecost, J. Dwight. "Daniel." In *The Bible Knowledge Commentary.* Old Testament edition. Edited by John F. Walvoord and Roy B. Zuck. Wheaton, Ill.: Scripture Press Publications, Victor Books, 1985. Verse-by-verse interpretation of the text.

Wallace, Ronald S. *The Message of Daniel: The Lord Is King.* The Bible Speaks Today Series. Downers Grove, Ill.: InterVarsity Press, n.d. Insightful thematic study.

Walvoord, John F. *Prophecy: Fourteen Essential Keys to Understanding the Final Drama.* Nashville, Tenn.: Thomas Nelson Publishers, 1993. Helpful overview of end-times events.

Some of these books may be out of print and available only through a library. For those currently available, please contact your local Christian bookstore. Books by Charles R. Swindoll may be obtained through Insight for Living. IFL also offers some books by other authors—please note the ordering information that follows and contact the office that serves you.

ORDERING INFORMATION

DANIEL: GOD'S PATTERN FOR THE FUTURE
Cassette Tapes and Study Guide

This Bible study guide was designed to be used independently or in conjunction with the broadcast of Chuck Swindoll's taped messages which are listed below. If you would like to order cassette tapes or further copies of this study guide, please see the information given below and the order forms provided at the end of this guide.

		U.S.	Canada
DAN	Study guide	$ 4.95 ea.	$ 6.50 ea.
DANCS	Cassette series, includes all individual tapes, album cover, and one complimentary study guide	59.50	69.50 ea.
DAN 1–9	Individual cassettes, includes messages A and B	6.00 ea.	7.48 ea.

Prices are subject to change without notice.

DAN   1-A: *Prophecy in Panorama*—Selected Scriptures
         B: *How to Pass a Test without Cheating*—Daniel 1

DAN   2-A: *A King on the Couch*—Daniel 2:1–30
         B: *A Blueprint of Tomorrow*—Daniel 2:31–49

DAN   3-A: *A Ragtime Band and a Fiery Furnace*—Daniel 3
         B: *Insomnia, Insanity, and Insight*—Daniel 4

DAN   4-A: *The Handwriting on the Wall*—Daniel 5
         B: *The Marks of Integrity*—Daniel 6:1–16a

DAN   5-A: *The Lions in Daniel's Den*—Daniel 6:16b–28
         B: *A Prophetic Collage*—Daniel 7

DAN   6-A: *The Final World Dictator*—Selected Scriptures
         B: *The Living End*—Daniel 8

DAN   7-A: *True Confessions*—Daniel 9:1–19
         B: *The Backbone of Biblical Prophecy*—Daniel 9:20–27

DAN   8-A: *Spiritual Phenomena between Heaven and Earth*—Daniel 10
         B: *Wars and Rumors of War*—Daniel 11:1–12:1

DAN 9-A: *A Prophetic Quartet*—Daniel 12:1–4
   B: *The End of the Age*—Daniel 12:5–13

HOW TO ORDER BY PHONE OR FAX
(Credit card orders only)

Internet address: http://www.insight.org

United States: 1-800-772-8888 or FAX (714) 575-5496, 24 hours a day, seven days a week

Canada: 1-800-663-7639. Vancouver residents call (604) 532-7172, from 8:00 A.M. to 4:30 P.M., Pacific time, Monday through Friday
FAX (604) 532-7173 anytime, day or night

Australia and the South Pacific: (03) 9872-4606 or FAX (03) 9874-8890 from 8:00 A.M. to 5:00 P.M., Monday through Friday

Other International Locations: call the International Ordering Services Department in the United States at (714) 575-5000 from 8:00 A.M. to 4:30 P.M., Pacific time, Monday through Friday
FAX (714) 575-5496 anytime, day or night

HOW TO ORDER BY MAIL

United States
• Mail to: Processing Services Department
         Insight for Living
         Post Office Box 69000
         Anaheim, CA 92817-0900
• Sales tax: California residents add 7.25%.
• Shipping and handling charges must be added to each order. See chart on order form for amount.
• Payment: personal checks, money orders, credit cards (Visa, Master-Card, Discover Card, and American Express). No invoices or COD orders available.
• $10 fee for *any* returned check.

Canada
• Mail to: Insight for Living Ministries
         Post Office Box 2510
         Vancouver, BC V6B 3W7
• Sales tax: please add 7% GST. British Columbia residents also add 7% sales tax (on tapes or cassette series).
• Shipping and handling charges must be added to each order. See chart on order form for amount.

- Payment: personal cheques, money orders, credit cards (Visa, Master-Card). No invoices or COD orders available.
- Delivery: approximately four weeks.

Australia and the South Pacific
- Mail to: Insight for Living, Inc.
  GPO Box 2823 EE
  Melbourne, Victoria 3001, Australia
- Shipping: add 25% to the total order.
- Delivery: approximately four to six weeks.
- Payment: personal checks payable in Australian funds, international money orders, or credit cards (Visa, MasterCard, and Bankcard).

United Kingdom and Europe
- Mail to: Insight for Living
  c/o Trans World Radio
  Post Office Box 1020
  Bristol, BS99 1XS
  England, United Kingdom
- Shipping: add 25% to the total order.
- Delivery: approximately four to six weeks.
- Payment: cheques payable in sterling pounds or credit cards (Visa, MasterCard, and American Express).

Other International Locations
- Mail to: International Processing Services Department
  Insight for Living
  Post Office Box 69000
  Anaheim, CA 92817-0900
- Shipping and delivery time: please see chart that follows.
- Payment: personal checks payable in U.S. funds, international money orders, or credit cards (Visa, MasterCard, and American Express).

Type of Shipping	Postage Cost	Delivery
Surface	10% of total order*	6 to 10 weeks
Airmail	25% of total order*	under 6 weeks

*Use U.S. price as a base.

Our Guarantee: Your complete satisfaction is our top priority here at Insight for Living. If you're not completely satisfied with anything you order, please return it for full credit, a refund, or a replacement, as you prefer.

Insight for Living Catalog: The Insight for Living catalog features study guides, tapes, and books by a variety of Christian authors. To obtain a free copy, call us at the numbers listed above.

Order Form
United States, Australia, and Other International Locations
(Canadian residents please use order form on reverse side.)

DANCS represents the entire *Daniel: God's Pattern for the Future* series in a special album cover, while DAN 1–9 are the individual tapes included in the series. DAN represents this study guide, should you desire to order additional copies.

DAN	Study guide	$ 4.95 ea.
DANCS	Cassette series, includes all individual tapes, album cover, and one complimentary study guide	59.50
DAN 1–9	Individual cassettes, includes messages A and B	6.00 ea.

Product Code	Product Description	Quantity	Unit Price	Total
			$	$

Amount of Order	First Class	UPS		
			Order Total	
$ 7.50 and under	1.00	4.00	UPS ❏ First Class ❏ Shipping and handling must be added. See chart for charges.	
$ 7.51 to 12.50	1.50	4.25	**Subtotal**	
$12.51 to 25.00	3.50	4.50	California Residents—Sales Tax Add 7.25% of subtotal.	
$25.01 to 35.00	4.50	4.75	**Non-United States Residents** Australia and Europe add 25%. All other locations: U.S. price plus 10% surface postage or 25% airmail.	
$35.01 to 60.00	5.50	5.25		
$60.00 and over	6.50	5.75		
			Gift to Insight for Living Tax-deductible in the United States.	
			Total Amount Due Please do not send cash.	$

Fed Ex and Fourth Class are also available. Please call for details.

If you are placing an order after January 1, 1997, please call for current prices.

Prices are subject to change without notice.

Payment by: ❏ Check or money order payable to Insight for Living   ❏ Credit card

(Circle one):   Visa   MasterCard   Discover Card   American Express   Bankcard

(In Australia)

Number _____

Expiration Date _____   Signature _____
We cannot process your credit card purchase without your signature.

Name _____

Address _____

City _____   State _____

Zip Code _____   Country _____

Telephone (___) _____   Radio Station ____ ____ ____ ____
If questions arise concerning your order, we may need to contact you.

Mail this order form to the Processing Services Department at one of these addresses:

Insight for Living
Post Office Box 69000, Anaheim, CA 92817-0900

Insight for Living, Inc.
GPO Box 2823 EE, Melbourne, VIC 3001, Australia

ECFR MEMBER

Order Form
Canadian Residents

(Residents of the United States, Australia, and other international locations, please use order form on reverse side.)

DANCS represents the entire *Daniel: God's Pattern for the Future* series in a special album cover, while DAN 1–9 are the individual tapes included in the series. DAN represents this study guide, should you desire to order additional copies.

DAN	Study guide	$ 6.50 ea.
DANCS	Cassette series,	69.50
	includes all individual tapes, album cover, and one complimentary study guide	
DAN 1–9	Individual cassettes, includes messages A and B	7.48 ea.

Product Code	Product Description	Quantity	Unit Price	Total
			$	$

Amount of Order	Canada Post		
Orders to $10.00	2.00	**Subtotal**	
$10.01 to 30.00	3.50	**Add 7% GST**	
$30.01 to 50.00	5.00	**British Columbia Residents** *Add 7% sales tax on individual tapes or cassette series.*	
$50.01 to 99.99	7.00	**Shipping** *Shipping and handling must be added. See chart for charges.*	
$100 and over	Free	**Gift to Insight for Living Ministries** *Tax-deductible in Canada.*	

Loomis is also available. Please call for details.

If you are placing an order after January 1, 1997, please call for current prices.

Prices are subject to change without notice.

Subtotal		
Add 7% GST		
British Columbia Residents *Add 7% sales tax on individual tapes or cassette series.*		
Shipping *Shipping and handling must be added. See chart for charges.*		
Gift to Insight for Living Ministries *Tax-deductible in Canada.*		
Total Amount Due *Please do not send cash.*	$	

Payment by: ☐ Cheque or money order payable to Insight for Living Ministries
☐ Credit card

(Circle one): Visa   MasterCard   Number _____

Expiration Date _____   Signature _____

We cannot process your credit card purchase without your signature.

Name _____

Address _____

City _____   Province _____

Postal Code _____   Country _____

Telephone (____) _____   Radio Station ____ ____ ____ ____

If questions arise concerning your order, we may need to contact you.

Mail this order form to the Processing Services Department at the following address:

Insight for Living Ministries
Post Office Box 2510
Vancouver, BC, Canada V6B 3W7